Leading Curriculum Development

Jon Wiles

For information:

Corwin Press
A SAGE Company
2455 Teller Road
Thousand Oaks, California 91320
www.corwinpress.com

SAGE Ltd.
1 Oliver's Yard
55 City Road
London EC1Y 1SP
United Kingdom

SAGE Pvt. Ltd.
B 1/I 1 Mohan Cooperative
   Industrial Area
Mathura Road, New Delhi 110 044
India

SAGE Asia-Pacific Pte. Ltd.
33 Pekin Street #02-01
Far East Square
Singapore 048763

Printed in the United States of America

Library of Congress Cataloging-in-Publication Data

Wiles, Jon.
Leading curriculum development/Jon Wiles.
    p. cm.
Includes bibliographical references and index.
ISBN 978-1-4129-6140-0 (cloth)
ISBN 978-1-4129-6141-7 (pbk.)
   1. Curriculum planning. I. Title.

LB2806.15.W558 2009
375′.001—dc22   2008021946

This book is printed on acid-free paper.

08   09   10   11   12   10   9   8   7   6   5   4   3   2   1

Acquisitions Editor:	Debra Stollenwerk
Editorial Assistant:	Allison Scott
Production Editor:	Veronica Stapleton
Copy Editor:	Ed Meidenbauer
Typesetter:	C&M Digitals (P) Ltd.
Proofreader:	Dennis W. Webb
Cover Designer:	Karine Hovsepian

Contents

Preface

This is a book about how to do curriculum work. Curriculum work is an essential function of leadership in schools because it is through the curriculum development process that we identify purpose, define activity, and rationalize decision making in schools. Curriculum work often separates the poor school from the excellent school. A school without a defined curriculum can be likened to a ship without a rudder; it lacks direction and is easily blown off course.

Many different kinds of people in a school can participate in curriculum work, including building principals, assistant principals for curriculum, department heads, teaching team leaders, and classroom teachers on special assignment. It is the activity, rather than the title, that determines who will provide curriculum leadership in an educational institution. Often, a person may be assigned such a leadership role without any formal preparation or real understanding. This book guides such people through the development processes that make up sound curriculum leadership in a school setting.

There are two distinct conceptualizations of curriculum leadership present in schools. First, there is a *static* or managerial kind of curriculum leadership that seeks to maintain and keep current all existing programs. Examples of static or maintenance functions are subject-matter reviews, accreditation reviews, and regularly scheduled in-service programs like the orientation of new teachers. Static curriculum leaders try to produce a degree of predictability and routine in the day-to-day operation of schools.

A second and very different kind of curriculum leadership is *dynamic* (leading). This leadership focuses on constructing new programs to meet the changing needs of schools and our society. Adapting the curriculum to the power of new technologies, for example, requires new and creative ways of thinking about education at a school site. Dynamic curriculum leaders establish direction, motivate people, and clarify the steps for changing. In contrast to maintenance leadership, the dynamic curriculum leader makes things happen; it is a visionary and forceful kind of leadership.

This book addresses both static and dynamic curriculum leadership, but is biased toward a dynamic role for those involved in curriculum work.

I believe that the degree of change being experienced by our nation, and the world at-large, demands that curriculum leaders be active and visionary. Upon completion of this book, the reader will understand both roles of curriculum leadership in a school setting.

ORGANIZATION OF THIS BOOK

The chapters of this book will take the reader from a conceptual understanding of the curriculum function to the actual construction of school programs. Following a general curriculum cycle of analyzing, designing, implementing, and evaluating, the reader will begin with defining purpose in school work and an introduction to the basic tasks of curriculum work. Chapter 1 and Chapter 2 define effective curriculum leadership and the basic tasks of curriculum leadership, aligning the reader to the development process.

Beginning with Chapter 3 and continuing through Chapter 9, the book provides the reader with detailed methods for bringing curriculum work to life in a school setting. Clarifying your destination by making the curriculum more purposeful (Chapter 3), building the school curriculum team (Chapter 4), and constructing the path for curriculum improvement (Chapter 5) are the prerequisites for successful practice. Detailed planning (Chapter 6), meaningful staff development (Chapter 7), and sound evaluation (Chapter 8) are key to the full implementation of curriculum plans. Finally, in Chapter 9, I provide insights from 30 years of field experience developing successful school curricula.

The reader will note various tools provided to assist in understanding curriculum work. In Chapters 3–9, a sample curriculum problem is introduced along with the identification of tasks required of the curriculum leader. Many of the identified tasks are illustrated by the 24 reproducible planning sheets in Resource A; these are forms drawn from real schools and real problems.

In addition to these forms, I have provided the reader with a master list of standard curriculum planning resources (Resource B), curriculum resource Internet sites (Resource C), some recommended resources for keeping up-to-date in the field of curriculum development (Resource D), and a glossary of terms to help the reader comprehend the literature of this area (Resource E).

As the reader proceeds through this book, the development process in curriculum work will unfold as a logical and clear way to provide leadership in schools. The reader will discover that curriculum leadership is a natural kind of activity in school settings, and that by focusing on school improvement, other day-to-day tasks of leading will follow effortlessly.

Acknowledgments

We thank our reviewers for taking time from their busy schedules to read the draft manuscript and to provide detailed and thoughtful feedback to us. We have incorporated many of their suggestions into the final version of the manuscript. Their thoughtful feedback has made this a better book. Our reviewers were as follows:

Sheila Fisher
Principal
Maria Weston Chapman Middle
    School
Weymouth, MA

Steve Knobl
Principal
Bayonet Point Middle School
New Port Richey, Florida

Beth Madison
Principal
George Middle School
Portland, Oregon

J. Dan Marshall
Professor of Education
Pennsylvania State University
University Park, PA

Lyndon Oswald
Principal
Sandcreek Middle School
Idaho Falls, Idaho

About the Author

 **Jon Wiles** is a highly experienced educator who has provided curriculum leadership to schools and educational agencies for more than 30 years. His specialty, reflected in this book, is the creation and implementation of curriculum plans. Dr. Wiles's work as an educational consultant has taken him to hundreds of agencies in more than 40 different states, and to service in a dozen foreign nations in Europe, Asia, Africa, and the Caribbean.

Dr. Wiles is the author or coauthor of twelve widely used books addressing curriculum and educational leadership. His text *Curriculum Development: A Guide to Practice* (Seventh Edition) has been used for nearly 30 years in colleges and universities throughout the world to train curriculum leaders. Other areas of publication by Dr. Wiles include teacher training, administration, school supervision, theory of change, politics of education, middle-grades education, and technology.

Dr. Wiles lives with his wife Michele on the northeast coast of Florida, and can be reached at J_MWiles@bellsouth.net.

This book is dedicated to curriculum leaders, worldwide,
whose daily work enhances the lives of young people.

Defining Effective Curriculum Leadership

Curriculum leadership in schools is pretty much what the individual leader makes it. There are many tasks associated with the curriculum development process and the leader is professionally responsible for sorting out and prioritizing this work. I strongly believe that curriculum leadership must be more than the management of existing programs. A curriculum manager would focus on reviewing materials, control issues, daily problem-solving, and encouraging a predictable routine from year to year. Such an orientation to the job is static. Effective curriculum leadership does all of those things plus establish new direction, align people and resources, motivate participants, and produce meaningful change for school improvement. In short, effective curriculum leadership is more than maintenance, it is dynamic in nature.

This distinction between just "running smoothly" and "responding to change" is very important on the job and reflects the general orientation (or philosophy) of the curriculum leader. The reader must ask, "Are we operating in a static world where schools are unchanging, or are we living in a dynamic world in which significant change is ever present?" The worldview of the school curriculum leader, static or dynamic, will determine what is considered a priority on a daily basis.

WHAT IS CURRICULUM?

Professionals working in the field of curriculum do not fully agree on a definition of the term. Some may see *curriculum* as subject matter or a series of written documents like books and syllabi. This definition is the general understanding of the public.

Over time, many writers in the field have defined curriculum as a set of school experiences. This definition is larger than simply "subjects," and includes what school people refer to as extracurricular activities. Lunch, play, sports, and other nonacademic activities qualify as a part of the curriculum.

A third, and more modern, definition of curriculum is a plan tied to goals and related objectives. This definition suggests a process of choosing from among the many possible activities those that are preferred and, thus, value-laden. The curriculum is purposeful and defined. Activities shape student behaviors.

Finally, a fourth definition of curriculum is drawn from outcomes or results. This position sees curriculum leadership as targeting specific knowledge, behavior, and attitudes for students and engineering a school program to achieve those ends. This is a highly active definition that accepts change in schools as a normal variable in planning.

These differences in the definition of curriculum are not idle or superfluous, but are important because they focus the responsibility of curriculum leadership. Such focus can be narrow or broad depending on the worldview of the curriculum leader. I favor a dynamic and adaptive definition of curriculum work such as the following:

> The curriculum represents a set of desired goals or values that are activated through a development process and culminate in successful learning experiences for students. (Wiles & Bondi, 2007)

CURRICULUM IS THE ESSENTIAL FUNCTION

Curriculum development is the essential function of school leadership. Whether this role is carried out by a principal, an assistant principal for curriculum, a team leader, a department head, or by leading classroom teachers, the curriculum defines all other roles in a school.

In recent years, classroom teachers have taken on much more responsibility for the development of curriculum at the school level. Operating under labels such as "teacher leaders," these individuals achieve advanced training and return to their schools to work closely with colleagues. This new pattern works well because the new curriculum leaders are also teachers.

Curriculum work is always value-laden; curriculum work is a matter of choosing from among many possibilities the set of values to be promoted in the classroom. We can think of the curriculum as a design for learning, much like the blueprint for a house. The curriculum is what we intend for students to experience. We hold expectations for the student because they experience the curriculum, and we measure curriculum success by student outcomes.

During the past 40 years, curriculum has focused primarily on results. Going beyond what is intended, curriculum leadership has determined outcomes that should be promoted and achieved by the curriculum. Selecting those things that are best done by the school, as opposed to the family or the church, the curriculum leader targets the learning experience of the student. Because the student experiences the curriculum, he or she can now do new things (read, play an instrument, get along with others, etc.).

Once the global goals for the curriculum are determined, the curriculum leader follows a deductive process to give more and more definition to the program. Analogous to an architect designing a house, the curriculum leader helps the school community and the teachers provide a highly detailed definition of what is intended for students. This definition includes goals, objectives, standards, programs, content, and even lesson plans.

As the curriculum leader defines the vision, his or her tasks transition from analysis to designing a comprehensive plan, implementing the curriculum, and, finally, evaluating the results. This sequence is known as a *curriculum cycle*.

These evolving roles for the curriculum leader include building a team to work together over a period of time. A school curriculum team is composed of individuals chosen for their roles and ability to contribute to such work. A larger school community, made up of teachers, administrators, parents, involved citizens, and local businesses, forms the human element of curriculum work. Curriculum work is always dependent on this human element for its success.

Working together, and coordinated by detailed planning, the team and school community translate curriculum intentions into nuts-and-bolts classroom activities that produce outcomes. A series of program sheets defining tasks, activities, responsibilities, timelines, and outcomes comprise a comprehensive curriculum management plan. Such program parts must be webbed together according to their importance and dependence. All members of the school curriculum team, as well as any member of the school community, should have full access to this bird's-eye view of what is happening. Change will occur more smoothly if those affected by the change know what is to happen.

Finally, as the teams implement the curriculum plan, the curriculum leader must monitor and coordinate the work being done. Such supervision is best done using a kind of "review and validation" technique that identifies, in advance, what is being done and what the work product is to be. Using the curriculum objective or outcome as a guide to managing curriculum work helps motivate everyone involved. Like a bathtub filling up, everyone involved will know their part and see the fruits of their labor. A successful curriculum development project will instill confidence and a winning attitude.

CURRICULUM MAINTENANCE

Simple curriculum maintenance at the school level is not easy, and can be a full-time job if done correctly. Any number of recurring tasks will determine the readiness of the school to deliver the planned curriculum as intended. Without tip-top maintenance, the curriculum can become distorted and even inefficient. In fact, in some schools, there is no overview of what the curriculum should be and no plan for maintaining the existing program. Figure 1.1 identifies some sample curriculum maintenance functions at the school level.

Among the most important maintenance functions for the school-based curriculum leader is serving as a conduit for information about classroom instruction. School leaders attend numerous meetings at the district level, and may also attend informational conferences at the state level where rules and regulations are promulgated. Getting this information to the teachers in their classrooms is vital for any modern curriculum. Most recently, for example, we are witnessing states changing their math and science standards, and this activity has direct implication for what teachers do with students in their classrooms. The school curriculum leader serves as a bridge for both the upward flow of inquiry and the downward flow of information.

Another very important maintenance task in any school is to ensure compliance with changing laws that govern education. Such laws may address the subjects in school, monitoring student achievement, class size requirements, or even the required resources for specific student populations. Exceptional students, for example, must be placed in classrooms under very specific conditions and this, in turn, can affect related decisions about hiring staff, building use, recordkeeping, and other items on a day-to-day basis.

Today, almost every state in the nation has achievement tests to measure the attainment of minimal curriculum standards. These standards, treated in greater detail in Chapter 3, identify in a general way what must be taught and what must be mastered by all students. The curriculum leader has to ensure that what is tested is, in fact, also being taught. Working backwards from test results, the curriculum leader can localize areas of low achievement using curriculum maps of each subject. In curriculum maintenance, where the school is deficient in achievement, corrections will have to be planned and implemented.

Keeping the school supplied with adopted texts and appropriate instructional materials is another task of curriculum maintenance leadership. In most states, textbooks are first cleared by a state textbook committee that assesses the text by a number of criteria (see Figure 1.2). For example, the committee will want to know whether the content of the text matches the curriculum standards required by law in that state. The committee will also try to determine if the text is relevant, supported by research, developmentally appropriate for that grade level, and so forth. Once adopted by the state committee, each district, and sometimes even each school, can select a text from the approved state list (Virginia Beach City Schools, 2008).

At the school level, the curriculum leader must help teachers replicate this adoption process by looking at things such as the alignment of the text with school curriculum requirements; the difficulty of the content level; the degree of reading difficulty; the accuracy, relevance, and authenticity of the content; and the multicultural representation as found in the school population. It is worth noting here that research has shown that the most common criterion for text selection at all levels of schooling is the physical appearance of the textbook. Curriculum leaders must work diligently to raise the level of sophistication by the teaching staff in dealing with such important matters.

Curriculum leaders providing a "maintenance function" in the school will also be responsible for all accreditation requirements. In most states, the school and the district is re-accredited every 10 years with an interim visit every 5 years. The importance of being and remaining accredited cannot be overstated. Parents and community members recognize accreditation as the single best measure of instructional quality. The workload to prepare for an accreditation visit can be unpleasantly burdensome for a new school curriculum leader unfamiliar with the process.

Keeping the school informed of district, state, and national initiatives

Ensuring compliance with state and federal laws affecting curriculum

Monitoring testing and the achievement of legislated standards

Adopting textbooks and other learning materials

Preparing for accreditation visits

Reviewing student achievement and monitoring recordkeeping

Developing a staff in-service program

Developing job descriptions and hiring qualified staff

Keeping up-to-date on current research affecting the curriculum

Figure 1.1 Sample curriculum maintenance tasks in a school

Supports state standards in the subject area

Has a clear, complete, and doable lesson sequence

Includes information literacy skills

Is grade- and developmentally appropriate

Incorporates a variety of learning strategies

Includes a clear purpose to be achieved by the student in any activity

Is visually appealing

Is current and free from special pleading

Figure 1.2 Criteria for state-adopted textbooks

Reviewing student achievement and maintaining summary records of such achievement requires the curriculum leader to have strong organization skills. In most schools, such records (state reports, district records, and test results) are kept by an office manager who is guided by the curriculum leader. Setting up a system of recordkeeping, and a schedule of such requirements, is an important maintenance task in every school.

It is equally important for the curriculum leader to develop a way to monitor how students are being assessed in the classroom. In most schools, the grading patterns vary widely from teacher to teacher. In-service sessions on this topic, and the expectations for student achievement, will contribute to a more manageable procedure in this area. Parents, in particular, will appreciate a fair system of assessment.

In all schools, staff development programs can help connect curriculum plans with classroom instruction. Assessing student achievement gains, for example, may identify some learning skills that are not being taught well. Once the weak areas of the curriculum are identified, the curriculum leader can schedule training sessions to improve faculty knowledge in those areas. It is inappropriate, and wasteful, for the curriculum leader to schedule regular in-service sessions without connecting them to school needs. Teachers and parents can be used to help identify areas of greatest need for additional training.

One of the most important curriculum maintenance tasks is to assess the deployment of staff positions. Faculty salaries and the physical facility account for 80 percent of any school budget. Vacated faculty lines are often simply replaced without thought about the changing needs of the curriculum. A long-range plan for any future vacancies is useful to develop as time allows. Part of this overall task is to develop clear and realistic job descriptions for the instructional positions at the school.

Finally, an important curriculum maintenance function is to try to keep abreast of existing research in the district and beyond (see Figure 1.3) Knowledge of current research will help the curriculum leader make instructional materials decisions, help identify new ways of doing things, and help answer instructional questions from faculty and parents in an authoritative way.

Together, these maintenance tasks keep the school curriculum rolling along and out of trouble. Obviously, the completion of such tasks will make the school curriculum more efficient and a great deal more effective. But the premise of such a maintenance orientation in curriculum leadership is that schools just don't change much year to year. I believe that in today's schools, maintenance will never be enough. A more dynamic role is required for successful school curriculum leadership.

DYNAMIC CURRICULUM LEADERSHIP

All schools are not equal in their ability to promote desired improvements. Although I recognize that basic curriculum maintenance is vital, I feel that curriculum leadership must try to do more than manage the status quo. If there is some kind of balance between maintaining the curriculum and upgrading school programs, the curriculum leader must always seek a greater and more visionary kind of role. The fact is, our world is not static and the curriculum in school represents our nation's program for preparing students to live in the future.

Although 90 percent of all schools use some form of ability grouping, research does not support this practice. The common argument for ability grouping is that it allows students to progress at a pace appropriate to their level of skill. Arguments against ability grouping include the self-fulfilling prophecy, teacher biases, segregation of ethnic or socioeconomic groups, and the stigmatizing effect on students. Conclusion: Too many negatives are attached to this practice and outweigh any gains.

Alternatives to static grouping would include (a) multiple placement criteria, (b) cooperative learning, (c) mastery learning models, and (d) greater use of computer-assisted instruction.

Best References

Oakes, J. (1985). *Keeping track: How schools structure inequality.* New Haven, CT: Yale University Press.

Slavin, R. (1990). Achievement effects of ability grouping in secondary schools: A best evidence synthesis. *Review of Educational Research, 60,* 471–499.

Figure 1.3   Summarizing research for faculty (example: ability grouping)

If we consider the changes occurring in our everyday lives, it is clear that the future will not be the same as the past or present. Communication technology and the changing nature of work, for example, call for major changes in the way we school children. The curriculum leader must be both visionary and skilled at translating such projected changes into school preparation programs. In this sense, the field of curriculum is like the "brain" of the school body; it is forever monitoring the environment and seeking a better way to serve the students. The curriculum leader is first an engineer (maintenance), but he or she must also be an architect of new school programs. Curriculum work is about programming and enhancing the lives of children.

Any number of tasks can illustrate the dynamic side of curriculum leadership (see Figure 1.4). What is common to each of these more dynamic tasks is the emphasis on planned change. The dynamic curriculum leader continually seeks to move from where we are in the present to an improved condition for our students in the future.

The dynamic view of curriculum work is that it is an active process involving the continual construction and improvement of school programs. Improvement most often means change. For such a view to exist and be accepted in the minds of faculty, parents, and school community members, the curriculum leader must facilitate a process of *visioning*. Advancing perceptions from the present to the future includes assessing common beliefs, tangible goals, and value priorities in school programs.

For almost 20 years, achievement standards set by national and state politicians have defined public and private education in the United States. Such standards are reinforced by serious testing procedures that focus on how the taught curriculum meets expected outcomes. Almost one-half of

Providing a vision

Moving beyond minimum standards

Tailoring the curriculum to the clients

Establishing authentic assessment

Building a working curriculum team

Engaging teachers, parents, and the school community

Planning for change

Managing the process of change

Using tools to empower curriculum development

Figure 1.4 Dynamic curriculum leadership tasks

all classroom teachers now in service have entered education during this 20-year period and accept testing and curriculum subject standards as "the curriculum." In reality, most such standards are a product of traditional school subjects, special legislative pleading, and low funding (the basics) for education. Certainly, such standards do not fully address any clear expectation of what students might need for their lives in the future. The task for the dynamic curriculum leader is to move the faculty and the community beyond the minimum standards and toward clear and larger goals for the students. Any number of techniques can be used to accomplish this intellectual transition, a topic addressed in Chapter 3.

For more half a century educators have spoken of "meeting the needs of students" and "individualizing instruction." More than 50 years of controlled research exists to document that individual students in school are not alike and that they have different strengths and intelligences. Knowing this, the curriculum leader must focus attention on how to best organize the content of curriculum to meet the needs of the client (i.e., the student). The planned instructional delivery of lessons is also a part of the curriculum (Goodlad, 2004).

As the curriculum leader redesigns the curriculum, he or she must draw attention to the expectations for the program design (the outcomes): What do we want the student to be able to do? It is simply unsatisfactory to state such expectations in terms of passing a test or being physically present for the 15,000 hours of instruction that each student will experience in school over 12 years. We need to know what the student will be able to do because they have experienced this learning design, and we need to be able to "see" this outcome in terms of tangible student behaviors. Our assessment of the curriculum must be observable, authentic, and real-world.

The curriculum leader who performs only maintenance functions may be able to meet requirements (reports, reviews, and standards expectations) without much assistance. But the curriculum leader who intends to define leadership as planning for regular change and school improvement will certainly need help. Teachers will be the primary source of assistance, but parents and community members may also play a valued role. Engaging these groups will mean forming a working team and honing their skills. Such social engagement cannot be avoided.

The actual recruitment of teachers, parents, and community members to participate in curriculum activities will call for a degree of "psychology" on the part of the curriculum leader. He or she will need to better understand motivation and the effect of work climates on teacher behavior. He or she will have to give thought as to the best or most effective communication mediums. The curriculum leader will have to construct teams using our best knowledge of small groups and informal leadership. Unlike business or military leaders, curriculum leaders will have to use persuasion and "power with" techniques to be successful. The curriculum leader does not have the authority to order change.

The curriculum leader will have to be skilled at developing plans for changing. The difference between successful and unsuccessful change in schools, from my experience, is found in the details of planning. Ways must be found to illuminate the problems and provide paths to solutions.

The dynamic curriculum leader will need to examine the whole notion of planned change. What must be done to get others to contribute to school improvement? How can the exchange of information be facilitated? How will any change effort fit into the larger organization of district or state education systems? These and many other questions must be addressed and strategies formulated. Dynamic curriculum leadership will require planning.

Finally, the curriculum leader who is dynamic will need to understand the many tools that exist to boost change efforts and empower the curriculum development process in schools. The skillful use of committees, technologies, assessments, and other tools will contribute to establishing a winning effort. Comprehensive planning will bring logic and order to even an emerging curriculum design. A "can do" attitude will emerge.

Both minimum (maintenance) and maximum (dynamic) curriculum leadership will be addressed throughout the remaining chapters of this book. The reader should note that the two styles of leading are not competing, but rather are reinforcing and interdependent. The basic structures of traditional curriculum work, maintenance, serves as a platform for the curriculum leader to address more challenging and complex activities.

SCHOOL LEADERS MUST ALSO BE CURRICULUM LEADERS

As odd as it may seem, all school leaders must be curriculum leaders in order to maintain their role. In many schools, the "status leader" (principal, assistant principal) is the leader in name only. The true leader in any school building will be that person who can mediate between organizational tasks and individual needs. Said another way, followers in schools get satisfaction from participating in curriculum activities to the degree their needs are met. School teachers, working with children in classrooms each day, either follow the planned curriculum or don't follow the planned curriculum, according to whether it is satisfying to them. If the teaching staff has not been involved in developing the curriculum they are to teach, or if it violates their values concerning teaching, the teacher may just shut the classroom door and follow his or her own dictates. For this reason, classroom teachers are the key to all curriculum work and must be fully and openly involved in the development of school programs.

Most curriculum leaders today are selected from the ranks of the best teachers in a school. In many ways, curriculum leadership is a lot like classroom teaching. It is the job of the curriculum leader to determine how to best involve all teachers in curriculum work and, in order to gain commitment, determine the needs of teachers. A new curriculum leader will rarely be successful if they try to "be the boss." Instead, using his or her knowledge from the classroom, the new curriculum leader will try to mediate between the "system" (the district or school) and the needs of classroom teachers. In other words, he or she will individualize the experience for the teacher. Curriculum leadership is almost always a problem-solving process.

It is important to recognize that leading must go beyond the school curriculum team and the building teachers. Community members, particularly those with children in school, are very interested in what goes on in a school. Remember, curriculum development reflects values, and a successful curriculum effort must occur within the general value structure of a community or resistance will soon be in place.

THE LEADER AS HELPER AND GUIDE

Throughout this book the author will emphasize that curriculum leaders must operate in an open, involving, and facilitating way to be successful. Unlike an army general or a policeman, or even a principal of a school building, curriculum leaders don't have traditional lines of authority. Curriculum leaders are staff members, with authority borrowed from those in the chain of command. Curriculum leaders must use persuasion and demonstrate competence to gain support and participation from others; they must help and they must guide.

In the long run, supportive or persuasive leadership (power with) is much more effective and natural than authoritative (power over) leadership. As the curriculum leader demonstrates the ability to organize, serve, and meet the needs of those in the school and the community, future leadership will be simple. The curriculum leader is helping those in the school and community to develop the program they want for children. This is a win-win situation for the leader, the teachers, parents, and members of the community.

What the followers in the school will demand from the curriculum leader is competence. Competence in the role of curriculum leadership would include working effectively with others, evidencing planning skills, being able to encourage effective communication among all parties, and delivering the results that have been projected through curriculum development activities.

ACCEPTING THE CHALLENGE
OF CURRICULUM LEADERSHIP

I would encourage the reader to accept the challenge of curriculum leadership in his or her school. The reader may feel a reluctance to step up and lead, to be the organizer, and this is natural. Many times I have heard new curriculum leaders say, "But, I'm really only a classroom teacher," or "I really don't know too much about curriculum work."

In fact, former teachers make the very best curriculum leaders because they rarely forget that the entire curriculum activity is ultimately about what happens to students in the classroom. Curriculum leaders aren't just making fancy plans; they are designing real learning experiences for students. Designing learning experiences, ultimately, is the job.

Embedded in the reluctance of some new curriculum persons to assume leadership is a faulty perception that because they have gained the title, they are the leader. In reality, the individual will only be the real leader in curriculum as long as he or she can serve the needs of those who follow his or her lead. In this sense, leadership and follower-ship are interchangeable roles.

SUMMARY

Leadership in the field of curriculum can take two basic forms. Leaders can focus solely on maintaining the existing program through scheduled reviews, controlled activities, and limited problem solving; or the leader can broaden the work by providing vision, organization, and motivation so that others may participate in school design. The author believes that curriculum leadership in today's schools must move beyond the maintenance or management function to address school reform for now, and for the future.

The tasks in both maintenance leadership and dynamic leadership overlap, and the minimal role of maintaining serves to support a more dynamic and future-oriented curriculum leadership role. In every community, and every school, local conditions will determine the ratio of these two forms of curriculum leadership.

END NOTES

Goodlad, J. (2004). *A place called school*. New York: McGraw-Hill.

Virginia Beach City Schools. (2004). *Textbook policy and textbook adoption process*. Retrieved May 3, 2008, from http://www.vbschools.com/textbook03.html

Wiles, J., & Bondi, J. (2007). *Curriculum development: A guide to practice* (7th ed.). Upper Saddle River, NJ: Prentice Hall.

Basic Tasks of Curriculum Leadership

Curriculum work in schools is central to all other leadership activity. The curriculum defines school schedules, whether to place teachers in teams or within departments, and even the kind of instructional resources needed in the classrooms. The overall curriculum design determines what is to be a part of that plan, and what is not, and the planned curriculum generally provides order to all of the parts of the program. The curriculum can be thought of as a master blueprint for student learning at the school.

As noted, curriculum leadership consists of both maintenance and improvement of a school program. In a sense, school leaders dealing with curriculum matters are like both educational architects and engineers. A long history of education provides a basic set of tasks for learning, all of which are common to students in every school. Changing conditions in the environment, however, require constant redesign efforts if the schools are to remain relevant and fill student needs effectively.

In this chapter, we will look at four basic tasks of curriculum leadership in schools: defining purpose, collaborating for success, providing the path to follow, and coordinating activity for the attainment of the desired ends. Later chapters will fill in the details of these four tasks and help the reader explore how curriculum activities define each of these important functions. Let's get started!

DEFINING THE PROGRAM

The term *philosophy* appears in most curriculum books and is often treated as the point of origin for school curriculum work. A philosophy in the context of curriculum development can be defined simply as a formal set of statements about the purpose of educating. There are many different philosophies in today's modern schools. Most accrediting processes, for example, require a statement of philosophy as part of a school self-study. After 30 years of experience working with schools on curriculum matters, however, I would *not* recommend focusing on detailed descriptions of belief systems as a starting point for school curriculum leadership. Instead, I suggest beginning by helping to generally pinpoint the priorities and values of the school community: Teachers and parents will have a greater appreciation for specific activities that will help them discover their general priorities, and these priorities can help define the purpose of the curriculum (Wiles, 2005).

It is important for the reader to understand that any curriculum always reflects the values of those who created it. Is academic achievement, for example, more important than the personal growth of the individual student? Should we be standardizing the outcomes of schooling, or creating a curriculum that has many different paths? Should we spend the same amount of money on each student, or favor some students because they have greater needs? Be prepared to find value judgments such as these at the heart of all decisions and tasks in curriculum work.

The first important task in defining the program of your school is to find the common beliefs held by persons in the school community (see Figure 2.1). If any of these common beliefs are opposed by teachers, parents, or the community, the school program cannot be completely successful. In this sense, curriculum leadership is not a process of telling others what the curriculum should be, but helping others to uncover or discover what they wish the program to be. To the degree that the community, students, and teachers buy into the basic premises undergirding the curriculum, there will be less resistance to change and a lot more motivation for improving the program. Leadership consists of helping others uncover the purpose of schooling (Jacobs, 2004).

Once revealed, these common beliefs, or unifying statements, can serve as criteria or filters to help the curriculum leader direct change, clarify objectives and outcomes, define the role of people working in the schools, and guide the selection of strategies and tactics at the classroom level. By contrast, when goals are unclear or there is no consensus about purpose, schools can regress to reactive and highly political responses to improvement. Such a broken-front posture is rarely effective in bringing about desired changes.

There are many ways to elicit opinions from teachers, parents, and the community members concerning what they think schools should be doing.

1. Hold discussion sessions using focus groups.

2. Write "we believe" statements.

3. Review school data to uncover patterns and priorities.

4. Sort goal statements by professional organizations.

5. Study research to see what is recommended for schools like yours.

Figure 2.1 Ways to find core values and beliefs

One way would be to have open discussion sessions with focus groups on topics of concern. For example, what do the various groups that make up the school community think about report cards or athletics in schools?

A second method is to have the same kind of groups create "we believe" statements about the process of schooling. For example, "We believe that all students are individuals with unique characteristics and abilities." Or, "We believe that teachers in the classroom should be facilitators of learning." Or, "We believe all students can succeed in school." Such statements, when gathered together, can describe holistic beliefs that most persons in the learning community can support (Kimpson, 1982).

A third technique often used by curriculum leaders is to have members of the learning community review data such as achievement test scores, attendance records, and student work products to identify strengths and weaknesses in the curriculum. Recommendations from such a process can serve as goals for both maintenance and improvement.

A fourth common technique is to have school community members sort goal statements in terms of importance. Phi Delta Kappa, a professional education fraternity, has an established set of goal cards that schools can use in this manner to prioritize curriculum outcomes (available from Phi Delta Kappa, 408 N. Union Street, P.O. Box 789, Bloomington, IN 47402-0789). The Association of Supervision and Curriculum Development, the largest organization of curriculum persons in the world, has Ten Valued Learning Outcomes that can be discussed and selected by the school community:

1. Self-esteem

2. Understanding others

3. Basic skills

4. Capability for continuous learning

5. Being a responsible member of society

6. Mental and physical health

  7. Creativity

  8. Informed participation in the economic world

  9. Use of accumulated knowledge to understand the world

  10. Coping with change

Which of these 10 goals for education do you value the most? Can you rank-order the ten goals and defend your selections? How would these choices affect priorities in the curriculum design?

Finally, curriculum leaders can use educational research to help others define goals. Many government documents, such as "What Research Says," (Taylor & Valentine, 1985) are available to schools. Also, tens of thousands of studies about schools and classrooms may be retrieved from on-line sources such as the Education Resources Information Center (ERIC) to help formulate goals for education.

It doesn't really matter which process the curriculum leader uses to define the school program and get meaningful planning feedback. What is important, however, is that the process is open, honest, and fully understood by others in the school community. To successfully conduct subsequent curriculum activities in a school setting, most members of the school community must be on board. I believe that talking about what exists, using any number of these techniques, is more productive than simply discussing formal philosophies of education. As the writer and philosopher Alfred North Whitehead once observed, "A merely well-informed man is the most useless bore on God's earth."

COLLABORATING FOR SUCCESS

One of the major errors of many curriculum improvement efforts is to plan without involving others. People are naturally resistant to change when they don't know what is going to happen or why change is occurring (Wagner et al., 2006). The need to involve others is especially true in schools when working with curriculum. Schools are everyone's business, and members of the tax-paying community, parents of school children, and teachers who deliver the curriculum have a right to be involved planning what will affect them. A second major task of curriculum leadership is to promote such collaboration for success.

Communication can be difficult in large organizations like schools. There are many natural and not-so-natural barriers to good communication, and curriculum leaders must work constantly to ensure that everyone understands what is being discussed or planned. With parents, for example, there are those who were successful in school, and thus have positive feelings about school, and those who distrust any leader of an educational

1. Avoid jargon and educational clichés.

2. Use several mediums to communicate with others.

3. Use group work to overcome isolation and build consensus.

4. Create favorable climates for collaboration.

5. Always be prepared when interacting with others.

6. Honor diversity.

Figure 2.2 Promoting successful collaboration

institution. There are natural language barriers dealing with simple and not-so-simple vocabulary. Nonverbal language, or body posture, can influence how people receive messages and therefore distort communication. Finally, there may be hidden agendas present as someone or some group tries to manipulate the curriculum development process for their own purposes.

As was the case in defining the purpose of education, I recommend complete openness in establishing channels for effective communication and collaboration with the school community. One of the first things educators must do is cut way back on the professional jargon that so characterizes our everyday talk in schools. To community members and parents, words like *individualize* or *compensation* have little meaning. A favorite word in the field of curriculum, *articulate,* refers to an upward passage of students from grade to grade (e.g., the curriculum has articulation problems). Community members and parents, of course, think articulation refers to speech patterns, as in "articulating one's thoughts."

The medium of communication must be thought about and selected for relevance to the school community. For years, school leaders have sent messages home with students and wondered why the PTA attendance was so poor. In some communities, e-mail and on-line bulletin boards serve well. In other communities, there is no substitution for newsletters and meetings held out in the community. The burden of finding an effective communication medium falls to the curriculum leader, and the success or failure of any school improvement may rest with how well that medium functions.

In working with teachers, school curriculum leaders will use a lot of group work. In schools, groups perform important tasks such as initiating activities, coordinating work, and summarizing progress toward improvement. More subtle in school group work is the need to find and build a consensus for action. The nature of school buildings, with each teacher in his or her own room, means that any teacher can shut the door and ignore curriculum mandates. The source of motivation for any teacher to participate in curriculum development activity is his or her belief that the change is desirable. Group work with other teachers breaks down isolation and encourages discussions about curriculum improvements. Opinions of individual group members are often influenced by what others are thinking.

The curriculum leader will actually be the group leader in many curriculum activities. In working with small groups of teachers, the curriculum leader must help create a favorable climate for sharing, help members to understand the group tasks, be prepared to help group members settle differences through inquiry, and constantly help the group see their work in terms of shared values. In fact, student needs represent the highest value in any school curriculum improvement effort. A useful way to settle differences of opinion about specific activities is to ask: What do we think is best for the students?

Unlike classroom teaching, which is by necessity done alone, curriculum leadership will consist of many meetings in which the various activities contributing to curriculum improvement are connected. Prerequisite to any successful curriculum meeting is an appropriate environment, a well-planned agenda, serious time management, and the appropriate materials and equipment needed by group members. Although such meetings may seem a tiresome activity, they are the "bread n' butter" of school curriculum leadership and related staff development.

Finally, it is important that curriculum leaders understand diversity in collaboration efforts. Diversity is a broad concept that refers to efforts to be more inclusive in all institutional activities and to strive to address gender, race, ethnicity, socioeconomic background, linguistic differences, exceptional abilities, variations of talents and abilities, and special needs in all decisions. The United States has always been a diverse nation, and schools are a reflection of the complexity of our society. Curriculum issues will often reflect general diversity issues and therefore present a challenge to curriculum leaders. Openness and fairness with all constituents of the school community will pay dividends in planning for all curriculum improvement.

PROVIDING THE PATH

Leaders in schools have more freedom than teachers and often more knowledge of resources and trends beyond the school. Because of this enlarged knowledge base, the view of how things might be accomplished may be clearer to the leader than the followers. One of the major roles for any school curriculum leader, then, is to provide a clear path to follow. This path is a product of a leader's vision, leadership style, way of working, clear goals, and an effective feedback mechanism.

In order to lead, one must have vision. Said another way, the leader must have preferences or priorities (values) in making everyday decisions about a host of things. Collectively, these many things form into a concept or idea or model of how things should be (Stogdill, 1974).

All leaders carry such thoughts in their head, but to clarify them for others the leader may use images, analogies, and metaphors to focus the vision. It is nice to declare you want your school to be number one, for example, but it is more helpful for those trying to follow if you define this condition further in terms of things you would like to see in the school. Number one may consist of many things, such as test scores, great student activities, parent–school relations, winning athletic teams, friendly student relations, and so forth. Specifying what "number one" means is essential to achieving number one status.

Research on leadership suggests a transaction that takes place between leaders and followers under certain prerequisite conditions (Lovell & Wiles, 1983). Among the truisms of this relationship, according to this research, are the following:

- Leadership is always a group role.
- Leadership depends upon the frequency of interaction.
- Status or title does not guarantee a leadership role.
- Leadership in any organization can be widespread and diffuse.
- The norms of the followers determine who may be the leader.
- Leadership and follower-ship qualities are interchangeable.
- Persons trying too hard to control others will be rejected as the leader.
- Leadership can shift from situation to situation (Lovell & Wiles, 1983).

1. Have a way of thinking about what is to occur (i.e., a model).

2. Be predictable in your behaviors—no surprises.

3. Make all procedures routine.

4. Use goal and standards to frame the boundaries of work.

5. Provide a medium for follower feedback.

6. Present curriculum design as an on-going process

Figure 2.3 Provide a path to follow

Leadership style results from a predictable way of doing things. Leader characteristics, like "being on time" or "being easy going," help the followers anticipate your leadership moves. Leadership is a lot like dancing; be predictable in your steps.

To the degree that procedures or ways of working are routinized, followers can anticipate what will happen on a daily basis. If the leader always seems to measure and count things, followers will see curriculum improvement through that lens. The organizational pattern of work allows followers to contribute efficiently and make wise choices.

Goals and measures of goals (standards) tend to organize curriculum work in the school. Just as the philosophy of a school defines the boundaries of the curriculum, goals and standards identify in advance how much of something is expected. "Our goal is to have high achievement in reading and we want the achievement to be greater than 80th percentile as measured by state testing." Statements such as this provide a measurable goal for the school.

Finally, the leader will need to be able to receive effective feedback from followers at all times. If the project is not going well, the sooner that is known the better. Some of the feedback will be through formal reports and tests, and some will be informal through discussions. Curriculum leaders should find ways to be available for such conversations.

COORDINATING ACTIVITY

The complexity of curriculum work in schools is always a little surprising to those new to the field. At a minimum, we are talking about the management of a large number of variables including space, people, time, and products. The curriculum leader must be highly organized, and this organization is the key to any successful curriculum work. To the degree those who are contributing to curriculum work can see what is happening and understand how their part is contributing to the whole effort, they will be motivated to make the effort succeed.

Teachers will judge curriculum leaders in terms of their knowledge and general organization in approaching work. It is vital, particularly in the beginning, that the followers see their leader as prepared and clearly organized. Being on time for any activity is important because time is the most important resource for any classroom teacher.

Curriculum leaders use a lot of planning tools to organize work and communicate to others about the overall effort. There must be, of course, a general overall blueprint or plan for promoting change. A skillful curriculum leader will display any such change as a gradual unfolding in a series of stages. Progress should be plotted point-to-point and set to clear time intervals. What is to be accomplished because of all the effort should be clear from the beginning of the planning process (Tucker & Stronge, 2005).

Leaders of curriculum improvement should be highly skilled at using graphs, charts, and visuals to communicate with others in the school community. The Internet provides curriculum leaders with a new and effective resource for communication about detailed projects. The public has become accustomed to learning about school activities on-line, so using this resource is key to successful communication.

1. Always be organized, prepared, and on time.

2. Uses the concept of *stages* in your overall plan.

3. Use visuals (charts and graphs) to report progress to others.

4. Use effective strategies to promote change in your school.

5. Clearly connect effort to outcome.

Figure 2.4 Coordinating activities

Curriculum leaders need to have a clear understanding about the change process in schools. Schools are unique organizations, in which the human element is all-important. The overall goal in any change effort is to gain enough consensus so that people are supportive and participate actively. Detailed strategies for changing are presented in later chapters.

The critical idea for the reader to grasp at this point in the book is that the leader will establish or design a way of working for the followers. Using a number of variables such as budget allocations, group and committee assignments, formal reports, development plans, and so forth, the leader will structure the way the school does curriculum work. Like an architect, the curriculum leader helps focus what is to happen. Once that blueprint is established, the curriculum leader next focuses on how to engineer or implement the construction of the desired school program.

THE LEADER'S ROLE

The reader will note that leadership in schools with a curriculum focus is unique. This kind of leadership is not about telling, or deciding, or ordering change (i.e, power over people). Rather, curriculum leadership is a facilitating process in which the leader works with others to find common purpose, build collaborative work teams, structure a way of working, and coordinate many complex activities (i.e., power with people). Figure 2.5 outlines this way of working in curriculum leadership.

Making the job of school curriculum leaders even more challenging is the fact that almost all curriculum work in schools occurs while school is in session and others are busy with their primary tasks of administrating or teaching. The activity can be likened to repairing an airplane while it is in the air! The curriculum leader must be a coordinator, a planner, a communicator, and many other things to succeed. Power, for the curriculum leader, will come from persuasion and getting others to help, rather than from title or control of key resources.

---

1. Curriculum leaders lead by facilitation, not telling.

2. Curriculum leaders use the power of persuasion.

3. Curriculum leaders promote curriculum change as natural change.

4. Curriculum leaders frame all tasks in terms of the overall plan.

Figure 2.5 The leader's role

SUMMARY

Curriculum leadership in schools consists of four basic tasks: defining the program, collaborating among all of the members of the school community, providing a path or way of working for others to follow, and coordinating activity leading to the attainment of the program desired. Most of this work is highly interpersonal and requires specific skills to make work successful.

The following chapters will address these steps in detail and provide the reader with an in-depth understanding of the necessary skills to make their curriculum leadership succeed.

END NOTES

Jacobs, H. (2004). *Getting results with curriculum mapping*. Alexandria, VA: Association for Supervision and Curriculum Development.

Kimpson, R. (1982, Spring). Employing systematic procedures in goal-setting: A matter of necessity, not choice. *Planning and Changing, 13*(1), 31–47. (ERIC Document Reproduction Service No. EJ262626).

Lovell, J., & Wiles, K. (1983). *Supervision for better schools* (5th ed.). Englewood Cliffs, NJ: Prentice Hall.

Stogdill, R. (1974). *Handbook of leadership: A survey of theory and research*. New York: Free Press.

Taylor, A., & Valentine, B. (1985). *What Research Says About Effective Schools, Number 1, Data-Search Reports*. West Haven, CT: NEA Professional Library. (ERIC Document Reproduction Service No. ED274073).

Tucker, P., & Stronge, J. (2005). *Study Guide for Linking Teacher Evaluation and Student Achievement*. Alexandria, VA: Association for Supervision and Curriculum Development.

Wagner, T., Kegan, R., Lahey, L., Lemons, R. W., Garnier, J., Helsing, D., et al. (2006). *Change leadership: A practical guide to transforming our schools*. New York: Jossey-Bass.

Wiles, J. (2005). *Curriculum essentials: A resource for educators* (2nd ed.). Boston: Allyn & Bacon.

Making Curriculum Purposeful

To many teachers, the word curriculum refers to a book or syllabus or a course outline of some sort. Without question, parents and teachers think of the curriculum as the subjects studied by students. Curriculum work, by this definition, would concern updating and reviewing the documents that students study in school. Such a mechanical definition of curriculum is even common among some school leaders.

To the degree that this is the common conception of curriculum work in schools, the curriculum leader will be saddled with a "maintenance mentality" from all who might be able to contribute to curriculum development. In a static world, where nothing ever changes, this perception would be acceptable. But in a fluid and rapidly changing world, such an outlook may be largely dysfunctional. Instead of seeing curriculum as a bunch of documents and text material that have to be updated regularly, the curriculum leader must help teachers and parents see the curriculum as a creative process leading to a comprehensive and purposeful plan for student learning. The degree of sincere participation in any curriculum work depends on this critical distinction.

There are a number of reasons why this distinction between a passive and dynamic view of curriculum is important. First, of course, we are living in the most impermanent society on earth. Change is everywhere in the United States, and we need to prepare our children for a world of the present and future, not the past. In addition, the curriculum in any school is value laden—it always has value priorities. We must acknowledge that this program for learning is going to do something to our students; it will change their thoughts, feelings, and behaviors in some way. Finally, teachers and parents will exhibit a lot more enthusiasm for curriculum work if they can make a meaningful contribution. Maintenance work can be drudgery, and defining curriculum that way establishes a sense of dreary obligation, a sort of "we've got to do it" mentality.

For want of a better word, we need to find the school community's beliefs or philosophy of education before we begin to improve the school curriculum. This doesn't have to be a stuffy process, but it is an important one: Establishing purpose is absolutely essential for the success of what is to follow. Vision is a prerequisite to action (Wiles & Bondi, 2007). Remember, curriculum development is a deductive process and cannot begin until the vision or big picture is present.

FINDING YOUR SCHOOL PHILOSOPHY

Determining the philosophic beliefs of a faculty and the school community is a matter of communication (Broudy, 1962). Although this sounds simple, it presents several challenges. Schools, by their common design, isolate teachers into self-contained classrooms. Communication between school and community is also limited in many schools and districts because no vehicles for sharing ideas have been established by the educational leaders. It is my experience that designing a curriculum without consulting teachers and parents is an artificial and unproductive process. Unfortunately, this happens often in our schools today.

TECHNIQUES FOR FINDING CONSENSUS

To make the most of curriculum work, leaders must act to involve others in determining the purpose of the school instructional program. This should be an interactive process in which individuals share ideas and seek consensus. Below are four techniques, cited in Chapter 1, for gaining meaningful input that can guide any subsequent curriculum work (see Figure 3.1).

1. Study philosophy statements and create you own.

2. Sort goal statement cards to find those most supported by all.

3. Use needs assessment data to determine what is, and what should be.

4. Have study groups react to questions about purpose and practice.

Figure 3.1 Techniques for discovering beliefs about education

Technique # 1

From neighboring schools or districts, gather 5–10 philosophy statements used in their last accreditation visit. These statements will be the first item in the regional accreditation report. Gather teachers and parents together and ask them to select or highlight statements they like or to add and delete from these statements to come up with their own statement. Do this activity in small groups and then have each group report on what they favored and what they need to know more about. Using poster board, display the findings of all groups and identify the common items from all groups. Consolidate these statements to create a "working document" that can be modified as time goes on. Note: Be sure to select examples that have a wide range of goals to consider. If you can't find such diversity in your area, there are many such statements on the Internet under the search term "school philosophies."

Technique # 2

Phi Delta Kappa, a professional education fraternity located in Bloomington, Indiana, has a set of cards that can be "sorted by priority" in small groups. Each group chooses or rejects the cards that they favor, and end up with 6–10 key terms that describe their priorities for education. Repeating the procedure above, have the groups list their top six descriptors on the board and discuss what seems common to all groups. Allow time for discussing those items not favored by everyone. Using the final set of descriptors, have the group put together a beginning statement of their educational philosophy. As an alternative, you can carry out this same process using the 10 valued learning outcomes provided by Association for Supervision and Curriculum Development, listed in Chapter 2.

Technique # 3

Use data gathered from a preliminary needs assessment (discussed later in this chapter) to create a profile of the student performance. The profile should feature test scores, attitude scales, notable achievements, school-based experiences, attendance data, absentee data, and disciplinary data. Ask teachers, and possibly parents, what they think about these early findings about the school. Solicit descriptors from the group about what these data seem to mean and what they would like to report about their school. Draft a preliminary statement reflecting the responses you have solicited.

Technique # 4

Have study groups at the school develop answers to a series of questions such as:

What is the desired end of an education?

How should schooling modify the character and activity of future citizens?

What can the school do better than other agencies or institutions?

What subjects in school are most vital in attaining desired ends?

What is our expectation for all students?

How do we deal with diversity in our student body?

Using this input from teachers, parents, and perhaps even students, you have now gained a first look at what the school community is thinking about the current educational program. Like an architect asking a client what kind of house they want, you now have an image and some labels that can be enlarged and detailed through additional and more specific questions. This input will serve as a beginning point for the development of a curriculum design at your school.

IF–THEN LOGIC

The information generated in the previous section is valuable because it provides a means for sharing, communicating, and thinking about what the purpose of education is at your school. However, the philosophy of education for your school is not complete yet. To completely define the philosophy, the curriculum leader must take the process a step further. If, for instance, parents say they want the school to know their child and tailor the curriculum to his or her needs, what does that mean? Or, if your teachers tell you that they believe that all children in school can and should succeed, what is the implication for classroom instruction? It isn't enough to jot down "individualize instruction" and "success for all" and say you have a philosophy of education. All that exists at this point are a couple of words for the marquee outside the school or sound bites for speeches to local service clubs in your community.

In providing greater detail about the meaning of the phrases you collected, we begin the construct a curriculum. For example, "Knowing all of the children in a school" may mean a mentoring program or a beefed-up guidance program at the school. Tailoring the curriculum to the child's needs or abilities may suggest the need for further data to determine precisely how great are the differences in ability and knowledge among children. The old rule of thumb is that there is a year of range for each year in school up to the eighth grade. This would mean, for example, that in the fifth grade there is a five-year range in maturity, achievement, reading levels, and so forth. Curriculum leaders and teachers need to take this range into account and create diversified learning materials.

If the teachers tell you they believe all children can and should succeed in school, you will need to gather more detail about what they mean by this. Form a subcommittee to define this belief. If this belief is to be made into a reality, there should be no nonreaders in the school. To reach this goal, we may have to look closely at how we evaluate and report student progress to parents. How does this observation relate to children with exceptional abilities in our school? If there are students who are not succeeding in our school, what is our plan to deal with this?

This "if–then" technique will lead faculty and parents into more and more detailed descriptions of their desire for a quality program of education at your school. Using outline form, a sketch of the program will emerge to be shared with the school community. When contrasted with the present conditions at the school, a development gap will begin to emerge.

THE ROLE OF STANDARDS AND BENCHMARKS

Standards are everywhere in education today. We have state achievement standards, subject matter standards from national organizations, and even text-embedded standards in learning materials. We also have what I will refer to as *benchmarks* or expectations for students in the curriculum itself. Standards and benchmarks are usually minimal attainment points that mark the "bottom" of acceptable performance (Drake & Burns, 2004). Many schools, not recognizing this, feel accomplished when all students reach the standard that has been set. Schools often feel accomplished when they have attained a benchmark such as a "counselor for every 500 students in the elementary school" or "10 books per pupil in the library." In reality, these are very poor conditions for operating a quality school program.

Such standards and benchmarks are often divorced from everyday life in the school. It is less important that an elementary school has a counselor than what that counselor is doing to reach the goals of the curriculum. If, for example, the parents hold as a high value that their child is known as an individual at the school, the math of 1:500 will suggest that the counselor must be a trainer of teachers in counseling functions. Otherwise, the average student might see the counselor 10 minutes every two months by scheduled appointments.

1. Standards are often superimposed by outside agencies.

2. Standards are rarely tied to global outcomes.

3. Standards, imposed by law, are sometimes unattainable by all students.

4. Standards are, at best, minimal attainment points in the curriculum.

5. Standards are a means to an end, not good in themselves.

Figure 3.2 Use of standards in curriculum

Likewise, 10 books for each child in school does not begin to provide the basis for an adequate library using a Dewey Decimal catalog system. Such a standard also sidesteps the issues of quality in selecting such books.

One last example can be drawn from school facility standards, which hold that the typical classroom for 30 students must be larger than 900 square feet. The reader will recognize that this is a 5 × 6 foot box for each student to spend 6 hours and 15 minutes a day in. And, all of that is before the furniture and learning materials arrive.

State standards should be added to those priorities in the school, but as a means and not as an end. Achievement in mathematics, for example, would be one mark or indicator of basic learning skill attainment. But is the school really concerned with mastery or use of basic skills? Do we really want test performance, or do we desire a future citizen who can use math in a changing world?

CLARIFYING GOALS AND OBJECTIVES

As the "filling in" process continues, the writing of goal and objective statements takes on new importance. Goals serve as organizers for program development (Mager, 1977). A goal of basic skills mastery might include (a) meeting achievement standards, (b) solving practical problems with mathematical solutions, and (c) thinking mathematically about the world around us. Objectives, by contrast, tell us how much performance we desire from the student. Some of the objectives may be cognitive, such as scoring at a certain performance level on state achievement tests. Other objectives may be affective, indicating an attitude toward a subject such as mathematics. Together, goals and objectives target student performance that is desired. We build a curriculum to attain the desired levels of student performance.

1. Goals are organizers identifying *what* we are doing.

2. Objectives tell us *how much* performance we desire from the student.

3. Taxonomies help us describe *what kind* of performance is desired.

Figure 3.3 Goals, objectives, and taxonomies

The various taxonomies of learning (cognitive, affective, psychosocial) may help us to find the words to describe the actual desired outcomes for these goals. Moving upward on the scales in the box below, we increase complexity and the degree of student participation.

Evaluate			
Synthesize	^	Characterize	^
Analyze	^	Organize	^	Adapt
Apply	^	Value	^	Practice
Comprehend	^	Respond	^	Imitate
Know	^	Receive	^	Observe
B. Bloom—Cognitive Taxonomy		D. Krathwohl—Affective Taxonomy		A. Harrow—Psychosocial Taxonomy

As we select words that define our goals (moving upward in each taxonomy) we are providing greater definition (i.e., targeting) and improving our ability to assess our curriculum's effectiveness in meeting our goals and objectives (Lorin & Krathwohl, 2000). In writing goals, and then more defined "enabling objectives," it may be helpful to visualize these desired outcomes. Can we, two or three years from now, show the goal and its parts to a visitor to our school? What would a "high tech classroom" look like? What would we see if our students developed art appreciation?

PRE-ASSESSING SCHOOL CAPACITY

In the goal stage of curriculum work, there is a tendency to overdo it. It's nice to dream of being in the top 10 percent of all schools, but moving from the upper half to the top 10 percent may just be unrealistic. It is best to work toward goals and objectives in stages; we plan to move up 10 percent each year (objective) with the goal of attaining the top 10 percent in three years (goal).

Knowing what is possible, and what is not likely, can be aided by conducting a pre-assessment or a miniature needs assessment at the school. Taking each goal and its parts (i.e., the objectives), the school curriculum team should determine what would count as evidence of having met the objective. Then, a data gathering session will collect the appropriate evidence, in its present state, and the team will judge whether to keep the goal or objective or scale it down:

Goal → Objective → Evidence → Status Report → Judgment → Decision

Goal: To obtain academic excellence by

    a. scoring in 90th percentile on state achievement tests in three years.

    b. having individual students recognized for achievement.

Objective: Students will achieve at the 90th percentile or better on the state achievement test by the end of year 3.

Evidence: School is in 59th percentile in reading, 62nd percentile in math.

Status: School is achieving better than 60 percent of all other schools.

Judgment: Goal is probably unrealistic unless over 5-year period.

Decision: Rewrite the goal to read "upper quartile in three years."

Among the type of data that might be gathered for making such a decision about the objective above would be the actual test scores, a determination of the distribution of scores in the school (how many lower quartile students), the support from parents for this goal, and feedback from teachers about whether this test profile is accurate for the student population. Making a pre-assessment is also important for providing attainable goals for faculty to strive for each year. If the goals are unreachable or simply ridiculous, the curriculum improvement process begins to dissolve.

ESTABLISHING A DESTINATION

As we near the end of this first stage of curriculum work, defining the program, the reader will notice that a pattern is being established for the leader. The leader is helping the school community contemplate what education is supposed to do. A purely maintenance role, refining what we have always done, or just meeting state standards, falls far short of understanding the nature of real curriculum work. Through sorting, prioritizing, analyzing, and deciding, a common reality begins to emerge. The emerging image is a destination for the school.

The leader is careful not to use words or phrases that inflame passions (e.g., liberal, conservative) or remain nebulous and unclear. The use of data to determine reality is consistent with the way our society assesses performance in sports, politics, and the economy. It isn't necessary to use judgmental words when describing a condition: simply report the numbers that reflect assessment of "what is." Leave it to others to interpret what the numbers mean.

The leader facilitates a process of goal identification and defines those goals with observable or quantifiable cognitive and affective objectives. Each objective further defines the curriculum desired by the school community in terms of student behavior. Because each objective can be validated (attained or not attained), the process of curriculum work becomes one of activating programs that meet objectives set by teachers, parents, and the school community. At no time is the curriculum leader the absolute boss in this process. Remember, the curriculum plan cannot be activated without those who help define it. Many a curriculum development plan has failed because of blue-sky goals, lack of detailed planning, not involving others, or the inability to be assessed as successful.

VALIDATION AS A CRITICAL ELEMENT

Curriculum in schools is more than a set of documents. In reality, it is a master blueprint for student learning, one that shows both what is intended and what is achieved. Curriculum work is the manipulation of the many variables (time, space, students, teachers, materials) to design a program that meets intended outcomes. Curriculum work becomes exciting when the school community realizes that it has the power to build effective programs for students. The curriculum leader structures a process so that this insight can occur (Eisner, 2002).

The school community cannot truly understand that it has built an effective program unless the curriculum leader has created a process of validation. Validation (counting, not judging) is important to the motivation of all people involved in curriculum work because it allows the curriculum team and school community to see how well they have attained the curriculum goals they initially set. To set and attain goals, and to see programs designed by the school community succeed, is the key to making curriculum development a purposeful activity. The process of going from a maintenance mentality to seeing a more dynamic role for all members of the school community is the result of wise and competent curriculum leadership.

SUMMARY

Curriculum can be a dynamic function in schools. School curriculum reflects the values of the school community, values that are formalized in statements of goals and enabling objectives. Taxonomies are used to define the emphasis in teaching and learning.

Effective programs result from the application of an "if–then" logic that provides an increasing degree of detail so that the curriculum can be defined. Standards and benchmarks give definition to a curriculum but should not be seen as "the curriculum." They address only minimal expectations for the school program.

Comparing goals and objectives to real-world conditions through a pre-assessment can establish a common reality for all persons in the school community. Stating goals and objectives in a form that allows validation will provide the source of motivation for those working to develop school programs.

Sample Problem and Leader Actions

Primary Programs (Kindergarten)

Activity	Actions
Programs for young children, preschool and primary, are vitally important to both the student and society. Whereas our knowledge of how young children learn and grow has increased considerably in the past 50 years, the support system for children (family) has declined markedly. School programs are being asked to compensate for this condition	**Provide support documents.** (Resource A—R16)
Most primary programs are constructed on a model of human development that sees growth as the mastery of tasks. Our models of development (Gessell, 1977; Havighurst, 1962; Piaget, 1959) provide reasonable guides for curriculum development. A recent research study of 23,000 primary students (the Childhood Longitudinal Study Kindergarten Cohort, 1994), helps to define natural development and the effects of nurturing growth. It appears that conditions of support increase learning in young persons.	**Support assumptions with model like Piaget. Retrieve this study and disseminate.** (Resource A—R19)
Preschool programs, and to some degree the first two years of formal schooling, include a number of components in some relationship or ratio: nurturing, skill readiness, support, and enrichment. The understanding of how learning occurs at this early stage of development defines the ratio of these program elements in the curriculum.	**Determine which of the four components are most important. Use pie graph to show relationship.**
In defining the program, the curriculum leader will need to provide a global statement of purpose, a data-driven rationale, and a design that will fit neatly with the existing primary programs in the school. The school curriculum Team may want to invite members of the community to participate in studying human development (birth to five) and relevant research in areas such as readiness, stages of growth, social influences, and gender in order to facilitate a common language for curriculum work.	**Form a study group including parents. Provide the study materials to the group.**

(Continued)

(Continued)

Activity	Actions
The statement of purpose might address school readiness, individual differences, intelligence (Gardner, 1994), and socialization requirements. This statement should be supported by information about the community, socialization opportunities, diversity, and early school performance in the district.	**Retrieve and enter relevant needs assessment data from district records.** (Resource A—R5)
The program will serve approximately 90 children ages 4–5 who do not have full readiness for school. The program will be divided into two distinct components. In the morning component there will be a formal education program to assist in the development of social skills, prereading, motor tasks, and enrichment. The afternoon program will provide child care for those parents who work and will address exercise and social skill development.	**Develop and share graphic showing the two parts and what is in each part.**
The establishment of this school-sponsored program will need major collaboration and communication with the larger school community since competing programs may exist in the private sector. Parents can assist in gathering data and in goal-setting. The strengths of the public program include costs to the parent, the qualification of the teachers, and the articulation with first grade programs in the school	**Identify the skills and show articulation with next grades.**
Teachers and parents may wish to visit the site of several existing programs in the area to determine the feasibility of any program component. Very important to the success of this program is the facility in which it will be housed.	**Arrange a visit and prescreen what will be observed.**
The early report to the school board should include a general philosophy, a statement of purpose, a budget, and a timeline for implementation. The budget will be dominated by teacher and aide salaries and the need for many instructional materials. Any philosophy statement should be simple, free of jargon, and emphasize developmental aspects of the preschool program.	**Send board member a 1-page outline and follow with a 3-5 page summary.** (Resource A—R4)
The path to implement this program will include several large categories, including goals and program components facilities, teacher selection and training, and major validation points during program development. Deductive logic (if-then) should be used to avoid the trap of focusing on classroom strategies before determining the desired outcomes for this program.	**Provide information in stages. Big ideas before fine detail.**
The coordination of activity in developing the Kindergarten program should follow closely the budgetary expenditures for this project. A simple task-cost-validation chart should help teachers, parents, and the larger school community follow the progress of this project. Like a bath tub filling up, the program will emerge from concept to defined program, through staged implementation, and final validation of all goals and objectives for the project. Opening this program on time should present few problems for the curriculum leader.	**Develop and share widely a task-cost-product chart so all can follow progress.** (Resource A—R14)

END NOTES

Broudy, H. (1962). *Building a philosophy of education.* New York: Harcourt, Brace.

Drake, S., & Burns, R. (2004). *Meeting standards through integrated curriculum.* Alexandria, VA: Association for Supervision and Curriculum Development.

Eisner, E. (2002). *The educational imagination: On the design and evaluation of school programs.* Upper Saddle River, NJ: Prentice Hall.

Gardner, H. (1994). *Frames of mind* (2nd ed.). New York: Basic Books.

Gessell, A .L. (1977). *The child from five to ten.* London: Harper and Rowe.

Havighurst, R. (1962). *Growing up in River City.* New York: John Wiley and Sons.

Lorin, W. A., & Krathwohl, D. (2000). *Taxonomy of learning, teaching, and assessing.* Boston: Allyn & Bacon.

Mager, R. (1972). *Goal analysis.* Belmont, CA: Fearon Press.

Piaget, J. (1959). *The language and thought of a child.* New York: Doubleday.

U.S. Department of Education/National Center for Educational Statistics. (2001–2007). *The early childhood longitudinal study, birth cohort (ECLS-B)* [Survey].Washington, DC: Author.

U.S. Department of Education/National Center for Educational Statistics. (2001–2007). *The early childhood longitudinal study, birth cohort (ECLS-B)* [Survey]. Washington, DC: Author.

Wiles, J., & Bondi, J. (2007). *Curriculum development: A guide to practice (7th edition).* Upper Saddle River, NJ: Prentice Hall.

Building the School Curriculum Team

Curriculum leadership is completely dependent on teachers and other members of the school community for the successful implementation of any program. The various members of the school community must share common values and communicate regularly to succeed in bringing about planned changes. For these reasons, as well as others, formation of a school curriculum team is critical to the success of all curriculum work.

In beginning this section, I should emphasize that a school curriculum team is not made up exclusively of teachers and other building personnel. As we shall see, involving community members and parents on such a team is a smart decision because they can serve as communicators to others beyond the school. Curriculum improvement is unlikely, for instance, if the proposed school program violates community norms or values or if the community is surprised by any change at their school.

SELECTING THE TEAM

The actual selection of the school curriculum team requires considerable thought by the curriculum leader because both personality and member roles will greatly affect how the team operates. Whereas there can be widespread participation on subcommittees for specific purposes, the formation of the school curriculum team is like establishing a brain trust for program development at the school. These will be the people with the "big picture" and the people with the logic to make the pieces fit. Any person who advocates for a special interest (the math department) or who is intolerant of others' ideas or groups at the school should not be considered for this role. Including such people on the school curriculum team may sabotage its activities.

The curriculum leader will need to select several teachers who are "opinion leaders" at the school. All schools have informal communication groups, and finding these leading persons can be as simple as asking the staff for nominations. Who would you go to with questions about our curriculum and who would you trust to make decisions about the curriculum? Drawing a line between the nominator and the nominee (a sociogram) will reveal who is most trusted and who is in communication with whom. The names with the most links are your school opinion leaders.

This process may take several rounds, but eventually you will place 2–3 teachers on this team. In addition, you will probably need other people representing various school functions: an administrator (if not you), someone from guidance or student services, and someone from the business office who is good with computers and numbers. Finally, you will need a couple of intelligent and trusted parents and at least one person from the business community who represents potential contact with other community resources. Assuming you will serve on this team, the number should not exceed eight persons.

A personal appeal to school service should be made to each of these individuals. They will meet often during the year and put in many hours as the curriculum development process accelerates. The individual knowledge of each person will grow as the curriculum development process unfolds, and group members will become increasingly valuable for that accumulated knowledge. With teachers, especially, this service should be presented as an opportunity to lead. Teacher leadership in schools is a relatively new and exciting development. I believe that this desire to grow as

1. Two faculty or staff opinion leaders (found by sociogram).

2. One administrator (the curriculum leader).

3. One student services person.

4. One business office person.

5. Two parents.

6. One business or community member.

Figure 4.1 Composition of the school curriculum team

an educator, to lead and be recognized, is the major source of motivation for experienced teachers. Curriculum leaders should recognize and capitalize on this desire in the classroom teacher (Wiles, 1993).

There will be, of course, a normal reluctance to get too involved in a process that may last from 2–4 years and having seemingly endless meetings. When you recruit the school team, be prepared to outline the way the curriculum development process will unfold. First there will be an analysis of the status of the school. Then there will be a design stage in which old things are made better and new things are created. The process will then enter an implementation stage in which, step-by-step, the programs will be put into place. Finally, there will be the validation piece in which proof of accomplishment shows the "winning pattern" emerging from all the hard work. Like a bathtub filling up, the school will be transformed. The school curriculum team will be instrumental in all of these successes.

In working as a consultant to school curriculum teams, I generally use the element of time to paint a roadmap for recruits. By Christmas we'll be at this point, by spring break this will be accomplished, and by next summer we'll be heavily into redesigning our programs. Don't be afraid to let your enthusiasm for this project show! Curriculum work in schools is impressive stuff if done correctly. It can be successfully scheduled and implemented.

USING COMMITTEES TO ACTIVATE CHANGE

Whereas gaining commitment for a long-term membership on the school curriculum team may be a tough sell, getting others to serve on various ad hoc (i.e., temporary) committees will not be as difficult. All teachers have experienced "death by committee" during their careers, and what they fear most is a massive waste of their time. Time is the most important element in all of education, especially for classroom teachers, and we must be careful to make teacher time count. Ad hoc committees meet, work, and dissolve.

In the curriculum development cycle outlined in a previous section, it is easy to see how the school curriculum team will lead the faculty from analysis to design to implementation to assessment. This school curriculum team will regularly create small ad hoc groups to gather decision-making data or to consider and recommend alternatives for improvement. The reason teachers and parents will want to participate in these groups is (a) most will be of short duration and (b) they will be affected by the decisions made.

The best way to handle membership on ad hoc committees is to allow self-nomination. If an individual wants to work on a specific piece of the curriculum, their personal needs pretty well guarantee sincere motivation. In fact, most well-known models of motivation (Maslow, 1987) hold that when a person's needs are met by activity, they are motivated to participate in that activity. The key to successful leadership, then, will be linking individual needs with the organizational tasks that satisfy those needs! (See Figure 4.2.)

When committees or even small discussion groups meet, it is important to define their function. Such meetings, for example, are inappropriate for just disseminating information. If you, as the leader, want to inform or teach others, use a memo or e-mail to pass along the knowledge. If, on the other hand, you wish to get people involved, small group and committee discussions are appropriate. Attitudes, feelings, and relationships are fine-tuned during any discussion as the individual is exposed to other opinions or positions on issues. Remember, the important part of any curriculum work is the implementation of a program, and the committee members must buy in if they are going to be energetic and responsible for the application of ideas in the classroom.

There are some fairly obvious prerequisites for a successful group or committee meeting. First, the time of such a meeting has to be leisurely in order to communicate to the participants that this is a genuine exploration of ideas with plenty of time to implement any decisions. Second, the meeting should be held in a place that is comfortable and free from interruptions (cell phones off please). Third, refreshments are very important for setting an atmosphere in the meeting. This notion of an atmosphere or climate will be expanded later in this chapter. Finally, and this may surprise the reader, the small-group leader should not be you. People considered "experts" tend to dampen participation of others. People learn best from "near peers" who share the same jobs but may have valuable experience to contribute or share with other group members.

1. Define the project by the time it will take because this is teachers' most valued resource.

2. Outline the cycle of development: analysis, design, implementation, evaluation.

3. Use ad hoc committees to boost participation and individual motivation.

4. Link individual needs to organizational task where possible.

5. Remember, "near-peers" are the best ad hoc committee leaders.

Figure 4.2 Gaining participant buy-in

SMALL GROUPS

Because most curriculum development activity occurs in small-group settings, it is vital to understand the dynamics of such sessions. *Groups* can generally be described as two or more people who possess a common objective. Major group roles in curriculum work include initiating activities, coordinating functions, summarizing findings, and assessing the accuracy of decisions that have been made.

The major enemies of small-group work would include aggressive members, people who block progress for their own purposes, individuals who feel the need to compete in some manner, those who "special plead" for their own needs, and any member who withdraws from participation without leaving the group. The group leader, then, has a kind of steering function to make sure the group is on track and productive in its meeting.

If the reader is to direct a meeting or delegate it to a responsible member, there are certain tasks that the leader must fulfill. First, in addition to preparation, the group leader must instruct the group about its specific purpose. Certainly, the first question in everyone's mind will be "Why are we having this meeting?" This instruction should include answers to questions of why, what, how, and when. As mentioned previously, the time commitment part will be of particular importance to members (see Figure 4.3).

A second important function is to keep the discussions on-task. Outlining possible steps, redirecting back to the main point, keeping the discussion objective and factual, possibly suggesting new ways to consider an idea, and summarizing progress are all contributions made by the group discussion leader. The leader should be ready to confront nonproductive behaviors from members such as attacking ideas or individuals, introducing irrelevant information, attempting to reintroduce ideas that have been rejected, or even downgrading the importance of the group itself. It is best to be up front and identify behaviors like these for what they are and suggest the group move on.

1. Instruct the group about its specific purpose.

2. Keep all discussions focused and on-task.

3. Draw together and summarize all decisions made by the group.

4. Continually monitor group progress toward stated objectives.

5. Select the group leader from the group membership.

Figure 4.3 Serving as a small-group leader

Finally, it is vital that the group leader draw together or summarize progress and decisions made by the group. Stating the group's progress toward its stated objectives will make members feel the time is being well-spent. If the curriculum leader sits as a participant in the group, a valuable role at this stage is to suggest how the school administrators might facilitate this process. The curriculum leader may be the only member with access to higher authority or knowledge of the budget process.

To summarize this often misunderstood relationship, the curriculum leader will establish a small group or committee for a specific function and turn over the group leadership to one of the members. That person will orient the group to its task, set the procedures for discussions and decision making, and draw the group to a productive conclusion within the boundaries of its assignment. The curriculum leader, who may or may not be a direct participant in discussions, then helps the group activate its ideas by linking them to the money, resources, and important people.

CONDUCTING MEETINGS

The conduct of a good meeting is a bit like a script or a "play" in sports. There are definable stages or steps, and these parts are necessary to the needs of those in attendance.

The beginning step is to clarify for everyone the purpose of the meeting. There should be precise objectives ("Because we are meeting, we hope to accomplish the following. . ."). Vital information, such as the meeting's purpose, the time, the location, and so forth, should be delivered to the participants in writing with plenty of lead time. An agenda should be prominent.

The meeting should convene as close to the announced time as possible, and the chairperson should provide an overview (roadmap) of what is to happen at this meeting. I am biased toward stressing the adjournment time at the outset and adhering to it each and every time. Consider everyone's time as super valuable. Teachers, especially, hate to have a meeting run over and leave them without preparation time for their next class.

It is wise to identify the audience at the first meeting and tell them why they have been selected to participate. If they represent a larger group (parents, the community), say so. Identify the materials you have provided and when they will be used. Look at the agenda and estimate how much time will be allocated to each section. Have an opening technique to get the group into the task. Be sure to try all of the projection equipment before the meeting commences.

The group leader should try to remember that the reason the group is meeting is to get all ideas out in the open so they can be discussed. If members don't participate, a handout might have been a sufficient substitute for the meeting. Deal with one item at a time, cut off the redundant debate, neutralize the dominator, encourage the timid, and keep the climate relaxed with humor from time to time. Although the leader may wish to employ rules of order, these should not be so strict as to cut off spontaneous discussion.

Finally, save time for the translation of ideas and decisions into action. Summarize the group discussion periodically, and in the end review what has happened and what comes next. Let each member leave the meeting thinking, "Wow, that was a very productive session."

CONFERENCING

Curriculum leaders in a school will spend an enormous amount of their time in conferences with administrators, district resource personnel, teachers, parents, and community members. These conferences will clarify communication, alleviate potential problems, and serve as feedback sessions for school community members. Such individual conferences are very important to all curriculum work. You can think of each person you meet as an emissary to others in the school community.

Like the small-group session or the committee meeting, the individual conference should be thoughtfully considered before it occurs. The general "script" for the leader is to hold the conference and have a successful conclusion. Finding a good place to meet, having clear time expectations, and identifying the steps to be taken should be shared with the person you are meeting.

When the person enters the conference space, you should try to sit about four feet from and facing the individual. You will first need to speak about something other than the business at hand to establish a social context for the discussion. This is like when a teacher transitions a class from

1. Follow a script, starting with social engagement.
2. Sit four feet apart and face the person you are meeting with.
3. Maintain eye contact and a slight inward body lean.
4. Be aware of your nonverbal body language and posture.
5. Limit jargon and clarify any complexities to the best of your ability.
6. Conclude the conference in a timely manner. Reschedule if necessary.

Figure 4.4 Tips for successful conferences

entering the room to getting down to the lesson. The curriculum leader needs to be aware of his or her body language. Good eye contact and a slight forward body lean will communicate that you are interested in your discussion. Try not to cross your arms, legs, or turn your body at an angle to the person you are speaking with because this nonverbal defensive body language speaks louder than words. Begin the conference with a statement of purpose, "O.K., we are here today . . . "

If you are meeting with a parent or a community member, remember to limit the educational jargon. In meeting with a teacher, keep in mind that all of this effort is always about improving instruction for students. Everyone is on the same side in effective curriculum development, and these conferences are to clarify, reinforce, or reward. Any breakdown in communication, because of a conference, represents a failure on the part of the leader. It's your conference.

All conferences should be concluded in a timely manner. To signal the end, change your tone of voice or stand up. Have your secretary call or stick his or her head in the door to remind you of your next appointment. If necessary, schedule another conference with the individual you are meeting with. Try to jot down what has occurred at this conference and send the individual a note summarizing the discussion.

OTHER METHODS FOR EFFECTIVE COMMUNICATION

The reader should attempt to clarify for themselves how various forms of communication impact the substance of the message. In today's schools, a variety of communication devices are used to maintain contact. These varying techniques all impact the message being sent; or, in the words of Marshall McLuhan, "The medium is the message" (McLuhan, 1967).

Memos, for example are an effective information medium, but lack the ability to let the sender know whether they are received, understood, or followed. E-mail, found in most schools today, is excellent at reaching all parties and can be responded to immediately. The downside, of course, is that no response is confidential (i.e., they can be forwarded) and they are sometimes lost due the volume of correspondence. Telephone conversations are a good personal device, but can be time consuming and must be repeated for large groups. Finally, the drop-in conversation in the classroom is very personal, but sometimes threatening to teachers and very time consuming for the leader.

The reader can begin to see the very important role of serving as the chief communicator for curriculum improvement. Effective communication is appropriate communication. Which of the mediums listed below seem best for the following tasks: (a) scheduling a meeting, (b) getting instant feedback on an opportunity, (c) explaining in greater detail a controversial topic, or (d) developing a procedure for working with several teachers?

Telephone

E-mail

Conference

Memorandum

Visit

1. Nonessential e-mail.

2. Scheduled and unscheduled meetings.

3. Drop-in visitors.

4. Ineffective delegation of responsibilities.

5. Lack of clear objectives or priorities.

6. Procrastination.

7. Telephone interruption.

8. Lack of personal organization skills.

9. Attempting too much in too little time.

10. Unable to say "No."

Figure 4.5 Primary time-absorbing activities

LEADERSHIP STYLE AND CLIMATE FORMATION

Leadership might be defined as the act of mediating between organizational tasks and individual needs. From this perspective, leaders interact with followers to get tasks done. What connects the leader and the follower is climate, communication, and leadership style (Litwin & Stringer, 1968).

In various studies of educational organizations, much has been written about *school culture* or the feelings people have about where they work. The subjective perception by those working in the school is sometimes called the *school climate*. What is different about schools, when compared to other organizations in business, health, or the military, is the degree to which human interaction is important. The interaction and communication between people in schools automatically establishes a set of perceptions that, in fact, govern individual behavior. Schools are exceptionally "human" organizations (see Figure 4.6).

People are attracted to work climates that arouse their dominant needs. The way in which climate affects school workers might be stated in terms of the following set of premises:

- on-the-job climates are made up of experiences and incentives,
- climates interact with needs to arouse motivation toward need satisfaction,
- climates mediate between organizational tasks and individual needs, and
- climates represent a powerful leverage point for promoting change.

Stated even more simply, the curriculum leader can establish a set of expectations in a school by arranging experiences and providing incentives for teachers. The leader can also develop an approach or pattern in working (i.e., a working style) that shapes the organization and sets a tone for interaction. Whether a leader is perceived by followers as business-like, creative, facilitative, or a taskmaster will result more from the activities planned than the true character of the leader.

This concept is so very important for new curriculum leaders to understand. The pattern of leader behavior (on-time, goal-oriented, open-minded, future-focused, laid-back) establishes a climate or way of working in the school. The leader can be purposeful in establishing such a work pattern by what he or she chooses to emphasize. This shaping of the organization will happen, whether planned or without awareness of what is occurring.

The leader new to curriculum work should consider what others see when he or she is interacting with them. Adjectives such as "organized," "on-time," and "student-oriented" will attract certain teachers who have similar characteristics and see the leader as someone who can assist them in meeting their own needs in work. You may hear a teacher say something like, "I really enjoy working here because they allow creative thinking at all times." This is a teacher who will not have to be motivated to think, because the teacher already is motivated by the perceived work climate.

What image would the leader like to project to others who will work with him or her in the improvement of the school curriculum? Like the individual conference or the committee meeting, this requires advanced thought.

1. Number of rules, regulations, procedures.

2. Responsibility: how much control the individual has over work.

3. Reward: perceived fairness in pay; being acknowledged.

4. Risk: general openness for taking a risk, without punishment for failure.

5. Fellowship: presence of friendly informal social groups.

6. Support: perceived assistance from above and below.

7. Quality control: emphasis on doing a good job and meeting goals.

8. Divergence: acceptance of different opinions and problem solving.

9. Team: the feeling of being a member of a working team; school spirit.

Figure 4.6 Variables that contribute to a climate

ACHIEVING CONSENSUS FOR SCHOOL IMPROVEMENT

Ultimately, the school curriculum team is formed to become an active and efficient instrument for the promotion of school improvement. This team of insiders will greatly affect the way others in the school community perceive the many tasks of school improvement found in any school building.

Scholars who have studied change in schools have observed that the process of getting a consensus for changing is much like an inverted "U" or a bell-shaped curve. Support for an idea begins slowly and then accelerates up the slope, rising up to a point where more than one-half of the persons support changing. At this point, often called the "tipping point," there is a significant change (Lionberger, 1961): A majority is achieved, and more people rush to join this majority.

In all curriculum work, the leader must work to gain a majority of the teachers (a working consensus) to support the desired improvement. In any school faculty, there will be those who are always supportive and those who are never supportive. In between, however, are those who will view the process from their own reality.

Using the many instruments of curriculum work (committees, grants, communication, reports), the leader must gain enough support to be able to implement any plan for improvement. Because schools are so "human" in their communication and interaction, and because teachers can simply shut their doors and not comply, much of what curriculum leaders must do is persuade others to follow. We will return to this theme in a later planning chapter.

SUMMARY

The school curriculum team is a vehicle for reaching all members of the school community in curriculum improvement. The school curriculum team represents the basic support element for the curriculum leader in the human organization called school. Members on this team must be chosen carefully.

Most work in curriculum occurs through group work, committee meetings, or one-on-one conferencing. This is where the curriculum leader will spend most of his or her time. Other methods of communicating with faculty and the school community should be carefully selected by the leader so the messages sent and received will be clear and effective.

Curriculum leaders need to understand the importance of school climate, which can serve to motivate others to participate in curriculum activity. The climate is subjective in that it is based on how followers see the priorities of the leader. The leader can develop a pattern of work, or a way of working, that sends a message to teachers. Once that leadership pattern or style is clear, teachers will have a greater confidence and comfort level for engaging in curriculum work in the school.

Sample Problem and Leader Actions

Intermediate School

Activity	Actions
Schools in America have designed numerous curricula for preadolescents in the intermediate grades, which include junior high school (7–9), the middle school (6–8), and the K–8 elementary school. Regardless of the grade configuration, the difficulty for designing school programs at this level is the diversity of the students. At no other time in school are the students so unlike one another. The range in achievement, social development, and intellectual maturity can be up to eight years in some classrooms.	**Gather data to document diversity and rationalize the design on the basis of development. (Resource A—R6)**
In studying the physical, social, intellectual, and emotional development of late childhood and preadolescence, most schools conclude that the curriculum must be highly flexible in its organization to meet the needs of this diverse population. Standard components of the organizational structure might include block schedules, teams of teachers, skill continuums, interdisciplinary instruction, enrichment minicourses, and student evaluation measures appropriate for the range of learners.	**Find some examples of nonstandard design with maximum flexibility to share.**
Many intermediate schools have failed to implement the desired program for preadolescent learners because they have not clearly defined the purpose of education at this level and also because they have not assessed the program thoroughly for results.	**Draft a philosophy statement for study.**
In creating a program of schooling at the intermediate level, the curriculum leader may want to begin with a pre-assessment of what exists. Traditionally, achievement declines in the middle grades and this alone may provide a rationale for change. Also, discussions of philosophy are difficult at this level because the child-focused	**Do a thorough needs assessment and exhibit any existing test score declines. (Resource A—R10)**

Activity	Actions
orientation of the elementary programs and the content-focused orientation of the secondary schools do not always mesh easily. The curriculum leader will find that focusing on data is better for any discussions about purpose.	
The use of curriculum management planning (CMP) techniques will be helpful in the development of middle schools. Study groups, for example, will meet and study and dissolve. Early groups might focus on human development, exemplary middle school programs, and needs of the existing program. Having identified these items in summary form, the committee would hand off the findings to a design group, who would then find the implications and translate them into priorities for the new school. Once these major design components are identified, a third committee would break them down to steps for implementation. A final committee might be used to monitor and validate the achievement of this plan.	**Create a curriculum plan after going through the curriculum cycle of analyze, design, implement, and evaluate. (Resource A—R13)**
It is important for the curriculum to map what is actually being taught in the elementary and middle school curricula and to clear out redundancy. For example, in how many places is "metrics" being taught? The final step is to then construct content continuums linking the elementary program to that of the middle school.	**Emphasize articulation in middle schools, as it is an important concept.**
A critical concept in middle grades education is balance in the curriculum. Too often, at this level, state testing or curriculum standards skew or unbalance the plan for study. It is especially important at this level to keep the long-term goals for the middle grades squarely in front of the planners. If–then logic will be used to ensure that the program developed is contributing to the ends in mind.	**Start with the philosophy and use deductive logic.**
The curriculum is defined by four major strands: the state standards for achievement, the importance of conceptual learning (interdisciplinary), a desire to help each student become technologically proficient, and applying learning in the community (service learning). Within these four strands, a number of organizational techniques are applied to activate the program. Included in the implementation strategies are block scheduling, multi-age grouping, cooperative learning, transitional sixth and eighth grades, mentoring, continuous progress content curriculums, looping, service learning, and problem-based instruction.	**Develop a visual showing the four parts and the enabling strategies.**
Because this curriculum design has so many parts, it will be necessary for the curriculum leader to clearly define the path for implementation. Using Program Evaluation and Review Technique (PERT), the dependence among the parts must be clearly shown. Each part of the total curriculum design (mentoring, looping, service learning) should be broken down into implementation packages (steps) and then wedded together in the comprehensive plan according to priority and prerequisite A special communication device for teachers, parents, and community may be needed to allow for an	**Use PERT/CPM to show how the program unfolds. Construct simple implementation packages in planning. Develop section on the school Web site to list events and dates for the community.**

(Continued)

(Continued)

Activity	Actions
understanding of the many activities in this change effort. Placing group plans, meetings, and activities on a special Web page, for example, would allow access by anyone to as much information as they need.	
A series of reports to district officials will be highly important to this project so that they might observe the return on investment. A project such as this will take several years to complete, and a record of the accomplishments will be essential to continuous funding support.	**Send quarterly progress reports to the board.**
Make use of public relations to boost this project. Feed accomplishments to news outlets and highlight teacher and community participation in this work.	**Send event plans to media the first of each month.**

END NOTES

Lionberger, H. (1961). *Adoption of new ideas and practices.* Ames: Iowa State University Press.

Litwin, G., & Stringer, R. (1968). *Motivation and organizational climate.* Boston: Harvard Business School Press.

Maslow. A. (1987). *Motivation and personality.* New York: Harper & Row.

Maslow. A. (1987). *Motivation and personality.* New York: Harper & Row.

McLuhan, M. (1967). *The medium is the message.* New York: McGraw-Hill.

Wiles, J. (1993). *Promoting change in schools: Ground level practices that work.* New York: Scholastic, Inc.

Constructing the Path for Curriculum Improvement

Now that all members of the school community are on the same page, the curriculum leader must help this group become a functioning team. Teachers, parents, and community supporters do not control the many variables involved in putting a plan into action, and rarely does any one individual see all the pieces of the puzzle. The role for the curriculum leader is to connect the parts and show the path for all to follow, which involves seeing the organization as a whole and recognizing how the various functions of the organization depend on one another. This planning function includes stating the vision, developing priorities, clarifying the steps, managing the many parts, and defining the scale of activity.

DETERMINING THE VISION

In Chapter 1, I spoke of the beliefs that undergird planning for school improvement. These foundational ideas determine both the purpose and the scope of work needed to improve learning in a school. A narrow definition of education might limit activity to scoring well on state achievement tests, whereas a broader view of education might include developing the whole person in each student. The goal for the curriculum leader is to produce a document that clearly states what is desired for the students in attendance, and how it will be done.

In Figure 5.1, the reader will find a reference to understand educational philosophies and their focus. At the most highly focused level (zoom in close), the school curriculum provides valued background knowledge to the students so that they will be prepared for further learning in life. As we back out (a wider-angled focus), the curriculum becomes more concerned with everyday living and the full development of the individual. The so-called "tight" curriculum would feature high degrees of structure, narrow and fixed learning materials, and a definition of education as something "we know." The more flexible view of education would feature greater variety in methods and materials and would further emphasize the application of knowledge in learning.

In orienting the faculty of a school for curriculum work, the goals will either be highly specific or more general in nature. A pattern of scheduled maintenance in curriculum work might include periodic reviews of each subject area and the use of backward designs to refine the instructional program to tested outcomes (Wiggins & McTighe, 2001). In the more general and dynamic approach to curriculum work, faculty assess the needs of students in terms of a changing world and redesign how learning occurs according to those findings. Most schools are certainly a blend of these two approaches in some ratio. A narrow curriculum might be called "perennial" or "essential," whereas the broader curriculum might be called "progressive" or "experimental." A completely open and flexible curriculum might be labeled "existential," because it would consider each student unique and each student would experience a personal and self-selected curriculum.

In Chapter 1, we saw how this distinction between the premises or values about education would set boundaries (i.e., the scale or scope) for further work. By these statements or declarations, the faculty is saying "these things are in our curriculum, and these things are not." The deductive planning process then uses general goals, objectives, standards, and other measures to further identify and define the curriculum. The purposes stated in the philosophy serve as the criteria in each stage of refining the curriculum, as they are used to determine what is and what is not in the curriculum.

Once the scale of the curriculum has been determined, a pre-assessment can determine the status quo and compare it to the often lofty aspirations of the envisioned curriculum. I suggest two techniques to accomplish this end: *developmental staging* and *outcome measurement*. In developmental staging, the faculty sees the change ahead by writing descriptors of common structures in the school (i.e., rules, roles, methods) across a three- or five-point scale ranging from the present condition to the desired condition (Figure 5.2). For example, if the faculty wished to

Philosophy Names

Perennial	Experimental
Essential	Progressive
Liberal arts	Existential

Definitions

Education as mastery of predetermined and worthy knowledge	Education as the use of knowledge for personal growth

Labels

Great books	Core
Standards-based	Broad fields
Disciplines of study	Individualized
Paideia	Interdisciplinary

Focus

High structure	High flexibility
Single textbook	Many learning resources
Subject learning standards	Multiple paths and levels
Centered on teacher behavior	Student as instructional focus
High degree of order in classroom	Relaxed atmosphere
Narrow and factual instruction	Conceptual or applied learning

Figure 5.1 Understanding school philosophy

individualize student progress reporting, they might envision varied and descriptive mediums using, perhaps, the computer to communicate with parents. By contrast, present practice might be issuing paper report cards using only numbers or letters to indicate progress. In between these two poles would be awareness of other possibilities, some possible experimentation with other mediums (i.e., e-mail to parents), and adopting a general model for the new curriculum. When presented comprehensively, these teacher-written descriptors reveal vividly areas in which work will have to be done and what must change.

If a pre-assessment determines that most parents of students do not have a computer with an Internet connection, of course, this vision would probably not be achievable. The faculty would then have to return to the planning board for other possible options.

	Stage 1: Present Condition	Stage 2: Awareness	Stage 3: Experimentation	Stage 4: Adoption	Stage 5: Desired Condition
The School Philosophy	Either no formal statement or a written document on file in the school office.	School staff share beliefs, look for consensus, restate philosophy and objectives in terms of expected behavior.	Staff begins use of goals as guide to evaluating school practices. Begin to involve students and community in planning.	Philosophy and goals used to shape the program. Formal mechanism established to monitor program and decision making.	Philosophy becomes a living document, guiding daily decisions. The program is a tool for achieving desired educational ends.
The Learning Environment					
Use of the Building	Only uniform instructional spaces. Little use of the building spaces for educational purposes.	Some deviation from traditional use of space (classroom learning centers). Possibly a complete demonstration class for bright ideas.	Limited building conversion (e.g., knock out walls). Begin to identify unused spaces. Planning for large learning spaces.	Development of a comprehensive plan for use of grounds and building. Total renovation of spaces.	Tailor-made learning environment that uses all spaces to educate. Building facilitates the learning intention.
Use of Materials	Classrooms are dominated by a grade-level text. Library with a limited offering, used as a study hall for large groups.	Use of multilevel texts within classroom. Materials selected after an analysis of student achievement levels. Supplemental resources made available to students.	Diverse materials developed for the students. Resource centers established. Cross-disciplinary selection of materials. More multimedia used. Some independent study.	Materials purchasing policies realigned. Common learning areas established as resource centers. More self-directed study built in.	Diversified materials. Something for each student. Integrated subject materials. Portable curriculum units (or carts). Heavy multimedia. Active learning centers.

	Stage 1: Present Condition	Stage 2: Awareness	Stage 3: Experimentation	Stage 4: Adoption	Stage 5: Desired Condition
Use of Community	Little or no access to school. Information about programs scanty. Trust low.	Some school program ties to community. Token access via PTA and media. School perceived as island in neighborhood.	Preliminary uses of community as learning environment. Identification of nearby resources. Use of building for community functions.	Regular interchange between school and community. Systematic communication. A network of services and resources established.	School program outwardly oriented. Community seen as a teaching resource. Systematic ties with service and resource around school.

Administrative Conditions

	Stage 1: Present Condition	Stage 2: Awareness	Stage 3: Experimentation	Stage 4: Adoption	Stage 5: Desired Condition
Organization of Student	Uniform patterns. One teacher, 30 students in six rows of five, in each period of each school day.	Understanding that organization of students should match curricular intentions. Some initial variations of group sizes in classroom.	Limited organization to facilitate the grouping of students. Begin use of aides and parents to increase organizational flexibility.	Full administrative support for a reorganization of students. Building restructured where necessary. An increase in planning for effectiveness.	Group sizes vary according to the activity planned. Full support given to eliminate any problem areas.
Report of Student Progress	Progress is defined narrowly. Letter grades or simple numerals represent student learning.	Recognition of broader growth goals for student. Use of philosophy to evaluate the existing practices.	Experimentation with supplemental reporting procedures. Involvement of student and parent in the process.	Development of a diverse and comprehensive reporting procedure for student progress.	Descriptive medium used to monitor individual student progress. Broadly focused evaluation. Team of teacher, student, and parents involved.

Figure 5.2 *(Continued)*

(Continued)

	Stage 1: Present Condition	Stage 2: Awareness	Stage 3: Experimentation	Stage 4: Adoption	Stage 5: Desired Condition
Rules and Regulations	High degree of regimentation. Many rules, most inherited over the years. Emphasis on enforcement and on control.	Staff and students identify essential rules. Regulations matched against the school philosophy.	Rules and regulations streamlined. Used as a teaching device about life outside of school. Increased student self-control.	Greater use of student and staff input into regulation of school environment. Rewards built in for desirable performance.	Moving toward minimal regulation and increased student self-control. Regulations a positive teaching device.
Discipline	Reactive pattern ranging from verbal admonishment to expulsion. Recurring offenders.	Staff analysis of school policies. Shift of emphasis to causes of the problems. Some brainstorming of possible solutions.	Establishment of a hierarchy of discipline activity. Begin implementing preventative strategies.	Design of curriculum programs to deter discipline problems. High-intensity program for regular offenders.	Program of the school eliminates most sources of discipline problems. The procedure for residual problems is clear to all.
Instructional Organization					
Staffing Patterns	Building teachers isolated in self-contained classrooms. Little or no lateral communication or planning present.	Limited sharing of resources. Some division of labor and small-scale cooperation in teaching. Information communication about student progress.	Regular cooperative planning sessions. Some curricular integration via themes. Students rotate through subject areas. Problems of cooperation identified.	Interdepartmental organization. Use of common planning time. Administrative support such as scheduling. Use of philosophy as curricular decision-making criteria.	Teaching staff team is working toward common ends. Staff patterns reflect instructional intentions. Administration in support of curricular design. Coursework integrated for students.

	Stage 1: Present Condition	Stage 2: Awareness	Stage 3: Experimentation	Stage 4: Adoption	Stage 5: Desired Condition
Teaching Strategy	Some variety but lecture and teacher-dominated question–answer session the norm. Homework used to promote day-to-day continuity.	Observation of other teaching models. Skill development via workshops. An identification of staff strengths and weaknesses. Some new patterns.	Building-level experiments by willing staff members. "Modeling" of ideas. On-site consultant help made available for skill development.	School day divided according to the teaching strategy used. Faculty evaluation of the effectiveness of new ways after a trial period.	Great variety of methods used in teaching, uses of media, dealing with students. The curricular plans determine strategy.
Staff Development	Staff development is global, rarely used to attack local needs and problems. Occurs as needed.	Staff identifies in-service needs and priorities. Philosophy assists in this process. Local staff skills and strengths are recognized.	Staff development realigned to serve needs of teachers. Opportunities for personal growth are made available.	Formal procedures established for directing staff development to needs. Staff development seen as problem-solving mechanism.	Staff development an ongoing process using available resources. An attempt to close theory–practice gaps.
Roles of Participants					
Student Roles	Passive recipient of knowledge. Instruction is geared to average student. Reactive communication with the teacher.	Investigation of new student roles by teacher. Limited hierarchy of trust established in the classroom. Needs and interests of students investigated.	Ground rules for increased student independence set. Student involvement in planning. Role of student connected to philosophy of the school.	Periodic review of student roles. Roles linked to schoolwide rules and regulations. Philosophy guides role possibilities.	Students involved in planning and conducting program. Increased independence and responsibility. Use of "contracts" to maintain new understandings.

Figure 5.2 *(Continued)*

(Continued)

	Stage 1: *Present Condition*	Stage 2: *Awareness*	Stage 3: *Experimentation*	Stage 4: *Adoption*	Stage 5: *Desired Condition*
Teacher Roles	Defined by the subject taught. Perceived as the source of all knowledge. Other roles peripheral.	Perceiving roles as suggested by the philosophy. Roles accepted at verbal level. Limited experimentation with new roles.	Investigation of new roles—trying on new relationships. Goal-setting for individual teacher. Skill development through in-service.	Administrative reorganization for role support. Sharpened planning and action skills needed to serve the students according to the philosophy.	Teacher role is defined by student needs. Teacher as the organizer of learning activities. Teacher talents used more effectively.
Principal Roles	Solely responsible for school operation. The boss, enforcer of all rules. The linkage to all outside information and resources.	Awareness of role limitations. An awareness of real leadership potential. A setting of role priorities.	Limited sharing of decision making in area of curriculum. Limited joint planning with the faculty. Review of existing policy according to the philosophy.	Role perception changes to manager of resources. Emphasis on development (active) rather than order (static). Increase in curriculum leadership functions.	Instructional leader. Administrative acts support the curriculum. Philosophy guides the decision making.

Figure 5.2 Developmental staging: Seeing the change

SOURCE: Jon Wiles, 1976, *Planning Guidelines for Middle School Education*. Dubuque, Iowa: Kendall Hunt.

Outcome measurement is a simple counting technique in which, for each goal area, the teachers decide the "observable" evidence that would indicate the presence of any successful program. Teacher preparation as a category, for example, might use the number of teachers holding an advanced degree as a measure of quality in teaching staff. If the goal were that every teacher in the school should hold an advanced degree, but the actual count shows only 70 percent of the teachers holding that advanced degree, then the difference is obvious. Shown comprehensively, this technique is effective in focusing conversation about what needs to be done, and what can be done.

In either case, the school curriculum team and the school community, in general, can become investigators in determining what needs to be accomplished in each goal area. This "filling in" process is deductive in nature, proceeding from a conceptual goal to objectives, to tasks, and so forth. Taking these goal areas, objectives, and tasks from the faculty, the curriculum leader begins to construct a bottom-up curriculum improvement plan. The faculty can clearly see how their part will contribute to the whole plan.

CLARIFYING THE STEPS

Most people new to the curriculum improvement process have a difficult time envisioning the many parts of curriculum work or how the various efforts tie together. It may be helpful for the curriculum leader to provide the followers with a schemata or flow chart of the entire process. Years ago, Ralph Tyler at the University of Chicago (Tyler, 1949) presented curriculum work as a cycle that begins with an *analysis* of the present condition, a *design* stage in which the desired changes are identified, an *implementation* stage in which the change is carried out, and an *evaluation* stage in which the progress is reviewed and verified. This evaluation step would lead back to another analysis of what to do next, and so forth. Many schools carry out a process like this every five or ten years for school accreditation.

Reflecting perhaps a slightly more modern vantage point, I prefer to use a *system* as the model to understand school curriculum work. Systems provide teachers with the critical concept of interdependence in organizations. By definition, a system is simply a grouping of objects that are treated as a unit. Systems can identify noncontributing conditions and bottlenecks that slow development. Traditionally, a system has three phases: the input, the process, and the output. This model fits nicely with the idea of curriculum work focused on attaining preferred learning outcomes.

In Figure 5.3, which shows curriculum as a system, the reader will note a progression from philosophy to goals, from goals to objectives, from objectives to program, and on to activities. It is important to point out that many curriculum development efforts in schools fail because the leader starts with an activity (e.g., adopt a text, provides teachers a workshop, buy equipment) without knowing the relationship of the activity to the goals of the program. Such a piecemeal approach to curriculum work is expensive and rarely productive. Open the closet of any classroom in any school and view the purchasing mistakes of the past! Seeing all of the parts in terms of the whole is not only necessary for successful curriculum work, it is also definitely cost effective.

THE USE OF FEEDBACK IN CURRICULUM WORK

As the curriculum leader designs a path for others to follow, feedback will be a major concern. Teachers, parents, community leaders, and even school board members will want to know if the path that has been suggested by the curriculum leader is the right path. Good curriculum leadership is often a product of good communication. In developing the curriculum implementation process for your school, the leader should consider using periodic reports and hard data to reassure followers that they're on the right track.

Schools, as institutions, are unusual places because personnel turn over often and there is little or no real continuity from year to year. A Navy ship, for example, has a record (log) of every important event experienced from the day the keel is laid in the shipyard. By contrast, ask other teachers at your school what was happening even three years ago at your school and be prepared for a shrug. If curriculum work is to be effective, there must be a substantial record of what has happened over time and there must be proof that the on-going plan is working.

Teachers and principals and superintendents and board members come and go; parent interest wanes as their children are promoted to the next grade. Only good records and reports can overcome such a transitory condition. Remember, too, that good curriculum plans often take three to five years to be completed.

In Figure 5.3, the reader will note that reports are written at each stage of completion. These reports are factual, clear, and intended to inform others about what is happening and why. These reports are a form of "taking the offense" in that they allow the curriculum leader to cut off conjecture, rumor, or purposeful disinformation intended to derail the development process. Such reports are also invaluable for new board members,

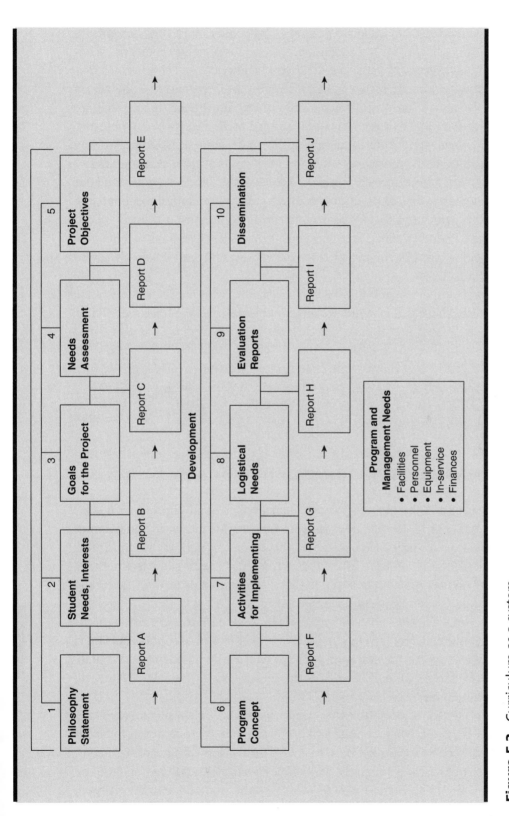

Figure 5.3 Curriculum as a system

SOURCE: Wiles, J. W. and Bondi, J., 2007. *Curriculum Development: A Guide to Practice*, 7th Edition, pages 98 and 112. Copyright 2007, Pearson Education. Reprinted by permission of Pearson Education, Inc., Upper Saddle River, New Jersey.

superintendents, or building principals who may start their job after a process has begun. As a compilation, the various periodic reports provide a permanent record of activity and accomplishments.

The reader may be wondering if writing such reports is really necessary. Obviously, writing a report every three months or so can be quite time consuming. But what must be avoided at all cost is the possible perception by experienced teachers that they have done this before. Nothing will eliminate the motivation of teachers quite as quickly as recognizing a process they have already supported previously. This is especially true if such an effort was without observable results. This feeling of déjà vu can be absolutely fatal to any project in terms of teacher attitudes toward change. Periodic reports will give your project identity, shape teacher perceptions about the success of the work, and minimize time spent selling the work effort.

I recommend using numbers in the reports wherever possible to state the case. There is a vast difference between stating "We have met all our targeted goals," and saying "All 10 goals have been met." It is a fact that Americans live in a data-driven society: We "count the votes," "know the score," and "are more than half done." When we measure, we use numbers, and the reports should reflect these easily grasped symbols of our achievement. For all practical purposes, words are vague and numbers don't lie.

MANAGEMENT AND TIME-DATING GOALS

Time is one of the most important elements in school improvement. This is especially true for a busy classroom teacher, for whom the question of time is ever-present. "How long will this take?" "When will we finish this project?" "Can I afford to invest this much time?" Remember, teachers are always assisting you in addition to their regular classroom job. They really have many other important things to do!

Results will also be on the mind of teachers, parents, and any community volunteers involved in curriculum improvement. Common questions might include "What will be accomplished if we do all of this?" "What do we expect to get for our labor?" "Is this change really possible?" "How will this benefit me?"

It is the job of the curriculum leader to provide a clear picture to followers of how and when change will occur, to show them the path to be followed. Feedback should come in many forms, including reports, action plans, numerical summaries, and time-dated goals. Managing by time and goals is one certain way to overcome the reluctance to be involved.

Any road map of change should be highly visible and easily comprehended. Charts, graphs, and other assisting mediums will instantly clarify the distance and direction of intended change (Wiles, 2005).

In Figure 5.4, the reader will see an overall summary of what is intended by one curriculum leader. Proposed as an *action plan,* this statement references

- the guiding documents (why),
- the areas to be improved (what),
- the new organization to be constructed (how), and
- the evaluation criteria (when).

1. Guiding Documents
   School philosophy with goal priorities
   Core program design with standards and validation criteria

2. Program to Regenerate Curriculum Elements
   Redesign guidance program
   Create new exploratory experiences
   Renew school curriculum map
   Establish interdisciplinary units
   Design new intramural program
   Articulate changes with elementary and secondary programs

3. Required Organizational Changes
   Simplify schedule to "block of time" model
   Redeploy counseling staff
   Reassess school grouping practices
   Use instructional spaces more creatively
   Redefine instructional loads

4. Training Areas and Staff Development
   Development of exploratory short courses
   Development of interdisciplinary units
   Review student evaluation options
   Explore counseling roles for teachers

5. Evaluation and Validation
   Creation of new student evaluation system
   Periodic reports to board using validation measures

Figure 5.4 An action plan for renewal

Numerical representations for the followers are superior to words in rationalizing any condition to be corrected or redesigned. In Figure 5.5, a simple graph depicts expectation and performance gaps for all to see.

Figure 5.6 uses numbers only to communicate to followers the range of diversity in the district, and to help teachers understand their school's relative condition when compared to other schools in their district.

NOTE: This class of 130 students shows declining achievement. There should be one year of achievement for each year in school. Those numbers that are shaded indicate students achieving below expectation. Note: In the first grade, 108 students are at grade level or below and 22 above expectation. By fourth grade, only five students are above the "one year of achievement for each year in school" expectation.

	Grade 2	Grade 3	Grade 4	Grade 5	Grade 6	Grade 7
5.0–5.9				5		
4.0–4.9			25	20		
3.0–3.9		15	15	30		
2.0–2.9	22	25	55	65		
1.0–1.9	18	60	25	07		
0.0–0.9	90	30	10	03		

Figure 5.5 Academic performance gap (shaded below level)

	Low	High
Enrollments	670	1389
Average Daily Attendance	83%	95%
Percentage of Low Socioeconomic Students	11%	56%
Student Mobility Previous Year	31%	70%
Ratio of Gifted to Exceptional Students	1/104	179/63
Average Score of Student CTBS Battery	36	80
Students Dropping out in Academic Year	0	22
Teacher Absences per Month	.36	1.27

Findings: The data confirm that a wide range of conditions and performance exists in the intermediate schools of the district. These statistics suggest that the quality of the intermediate school experience in this district may depend on the student assignment pattern. Efforts should be made to equalize programs and performance of the individual schools in the district.

Figure 5.6 Comparing schools in the same district. CTBS = *Comprehensive Test of Basic Skills*

Finally, in Figure 5.7, training dates are displayed to show various groups involved in a change project when their group is scheduled to receive staff development. This display also communicates that the dates for any one group may be influenced by many other groups needing similar training, or why one group is trained before another.

	August		September			October		November			December	
Group	25	27	6	13	20	17	23	4	15	23	6	9
Leadership	x		x					x			x	
Principals		x				x			x			
APC		x				x		x				
Visitations					x							
Board	x										x	
SCT		x			x							x
Teachers		x			x	x		x				
Parents			x					x				

Figure 5.7 Training dates. *APC* = assistant principal for curriculum; *SCT* = school curriculum team.

SOURCE: Wiles, J., and Bondi, J., 1986, *Making Middle Schools Work*, Figure 21, page 36. Association for Supervision and Curriculum Development (ASCD), Alexandria, Virginia. Copyright 1986 by ASCD. Used with Permission.

Now that each participant can place his or her role in the context of the overall effort, and fully understanding how long he or she will be involved, attention will shift to results expected. The leader can easily create a calendar of activity wedded to validation of progress: For example, "By January our staff will be trained." "We will be opening the new computer labs in April."

This linking of activity to outcome has appeared under many names in the curriculum literature. In the 1970s, people in the field referred to such expectations as *accountability*. In the 1980s, the literature spoke about *outcome-based education*. In the 1990s and into the early 21st century, the key phrase was *standards-based education*. Regardless of what it is called in your district, or at your school, there is a clear connection between any curriculum activity and some result. Curriculum leaders will benefit from making this connection crystal clear to those being asked to participate in the labor intensive process of improving school programs for students.

STANDARDS AS BOUNDARIES, NOT GOALS

Over the past twenty years, due to all of the standards and testing imposed on education, some schools have lost sight of curriculum improvement as a dynamic process. It is common today to hear teachers refer to curriculum standards or state testing as "the curriculum." The author would urge the leader to separate these two items, testing and the curriculum, as quickly as possible for the faculty.

Standards are nothing but compilations of notions about what constitutes learning in a subject area. They are usually not comprehensive and are often preceded by the word "minimum" (standards). As such, standards represent proposed boundaries on the curriculum and not goals for student learning per se. Standards may be items to be learned, quite divorced from the larger purpose of educating students or intended usage of these lessons in the future. In working with teachers, standards and state test programs should be presented as minimum requirements rather than as the curriculum.

Curriculum leaders can help stretch the faculty member who seems captivated by state testing by insisting that the faculty place any standard in a larger goal area. Ask the faculty: "Which area does the standard contribute to in our curriculum?" The faculty can also be asked to give examples of an application of the standard if they are used in lesson planning. This action will influence how the standard is treated in the classroom lesson plans.

SUMMARY

Curriculum leaders must assist all members of the school curriculum team in understanding any intended change in the learning program of the school. Like a puzzle, the parts must be assembled and placed in a pattern that can be easily understood by all. The curriculum leader must provide a path for improving the curriculum prior to commencing work.

To find a direction for such a path, curriculum leaders can use a process of envisioning where the scope of the curriculum is agreed on. Outcome measures, developmental staging, and other techniques can clarify the scale of the curriculum for participants. Using if–then logic, the group can fill in the difference between status and desired conditions.

Perceiving state learning standards as the curriculum will delay meaningful change. To overcome such a preoccupation, ask teachers to activate the standards in their lesson plans by attaching them to more general goals for the subject.

An important task for the leader is to clarify the steps that will lead the group from where they are to where they want to be. Cycles and systems displays often prove useful in organizing these steps.

Periodic reports distributed to all involved can illuminate the path and show measures of progress. Key questions for participants will be "How long will this take?" and "What do we expect?" Displays using numbers, graphs showing relationships, and calendars indicating events and time will further clarify the path to change.

The curriculum leader must be clear in differentiating goals and standards. Standards should be presented as low-level boundaries—a minimal curriculum. Goals should be related to a rationale for educating and expectations for usage by students.

Sample Problem and Leader Actions

Secondary Technology

Activity	Actions
The world of knowledge acquisition has changed dramatically since the arrival of Internet access in the mid-nineties. This single tool has raised troubling questions about the very need of schools as a place to learn and access to high-quality and current knowledge for all sorts of uses. Nowhere has this pressure been felt more than in the secondary schools.	**Define the role of knowledge in school learning.** (Resource A—R8)
It used to be that small schools were considered to be disadvantaged because they did not have the size to hire teachers for all subjects. Today, most school subjects are totally accessible on the Internet and some states, like Florida, have developed virtual high schools (Florida Virtual School—10,000 students) that provide high quality learning experiences. More than 50 accredited universities offer virtual degree programs through the doctoral level.	**Determine exactly what it is that technology can do better than the traditional school.**
Our schools face competition from the home school movement, in which some two million students are currently learning without coming to school. Hundreds of companies have been established to service these students. Curriculum leaders will have to acknowledge and respond to these trends or accept an increasing degree of irrelevance in today's high-tech world.	**Prepare to hear these arguments from taxpayers.**
Many schools and districts have reacted to the new learning technologies like consumers, buying wave after wave of the latest computers and learning aids. In many cases, such behavior has exhausted the budgets of the institutions, and skewed or unbalanced the curriculum of schools.	**Gather data about the existing conditions, such as the number and kind of technologies available.**

Activity	Actions
It is a fact that expenditures for computers in schools are actually declining as this book is written. Any curriculum work calling for the acquisition of technology must begin with a clear definition of the purpose of the work.	**Form a study group to define how to gather the data relating to technological expenditures.**
Curriculum workers in today's schools may be asked to develop new curricula for any of the following purposes: • creating new structures for learning and communicating, • designing new facilities with advanced learning systems, • allocating resources for teacher technological training, • using technology to apply knowledge in the real world, • finding and rewarding a new kind of teaching force, • networking teachers and parents, • allocating large sums of start-up capital for new programs.	**Become proactive by conducting a study of best uses of technology in schools.**
The history of technology in schools in the United States began with early computers (1980s) being used for skill acquisition and drill. These computers were soon moved into laboratories that looked just like standard classrooms. Schools initially had difficulty understanding the opportunity provided by the Internet to individualize instruction using computers. Standards, and security concerns, left most schools unable to do more than upgrade equipment, and that proved stressful to budgets.	**Determine the best cost-benefit use of technology in the district.**
When considering using technology in schools, begin by asking the question, "What can we do better using technology?" Certainly, any routine tasks such as scheduling and grade reports would fall into this category. But the real answer to this question is that the new and interactive technologies promise to help teachers individualize instruction. Just as all of the world's telephones have a separate number, each student in school can experience a unique curriculum using today's technology A teacher can effectively supervise about 10 students, but to keep track of 150 different students a day in a high school is impossible. Computers can do this.	**Prepare a five-year budget projection for a school. Determine what outcomes can be promised using the new technologies.**
The home-school movement has grown with the increased use of computers in the United States. Parents have learned that most school resources are available on-line and that each student can have a different course of study. Every day new companies emerge to service these students. Public and private schools can learn from the experience of home schooling by experimenting with the various applications of technology in the classroom.	**Find out what can be learned from the success of the home-school movement.**

(Continued)

(Continued)

Activity	Actions
To assess how to apply technology in the school, first determine the degree and kind of use currently present. Equipment needs to be inventoried, teacher knowledge and use of technology assessed, and an honest figure on how much is currently being spent on new technologies determined.	**Pre-assess home and school use.**
A survey of teachers, students, parents, and community leaders can help narrow the range of possible uses. Within the budget currently allocated to supporting technology in the school, several promising ideas that can be funded should be selected. Rather than jumping into the purchase of some "system of learning" or a large purchase of equipment, the process begins with exploration. Remember the defining question is "What can we do better using the new technologies?"	**Begin a pilot project with the help of the community.**
Because curriculum work using technology challenges many of the traditional values in schools (e.g., the role of teachers), it is best to establish a "no fail" program in which teachers will be invited to try out ideas without any real expectations for results.	**Establish mini-grants for teachers.** (Resource A—R20)
Once a series of experiments have been established, the curriculum leader should allow the school curriculum team to identify promising themes that will lead into a design stage. Here, a group of small projects will target some desired outcome. The sum of these goal areas (e.g., improve library usage using technology) will form the backbone of a long-term technology thrust in the school. Items will need to be prioritized and budgeted using the Program Evaluation and Review Technique (PERT). It is important for the curriculum leader to keep the many small projects focused on the larger goal of using technology selectively to improve instruction. Decisions about software, equipment, and teacher training should always follow the conceptual process.	**Allow the school curriculum team to assess projects.** **Create PERT to show the project relationships.**

END NOTES

Tyler, R. (1949). *Basic principles of curriculum and instruction.* Chicago: University of Chicago Press.

Wiggins, G., & McTighe, J. (2001). *Understanding by design.* Englewood Cliffs, NJ: Prentice Hall.

Wiles, J. (2005). *Curriculum essentials: A resource for educators* (2nd ed.). Boston: Allyn & Bacon.

Detailed Planning to Implement Change

To be effective at the classroom level, curriculum planning must address the details of everyday teaching and learning. It simply is not sufficient to hope that a goal like "individualizing instruction" can become embedded in classroom instruction without specific and detailed planning. Such planning must incorporate the nuts and bolts of teaching such as content, concepts, basic skills, standards, and sequencing of learning. Key to communication about such things is an unambiguous map of what is actually occurring at the school. Mapping the curriculum, aligning the curriculum, and tying the curriculum to standards and other learning outcomes can serve as important steps to meaningful curriculum improvement.

CURRICULUM MAPPING

A reality in most schools is that teachers, even the best teachers, don't always follow the curriculum. There are many legitimate reasons for this fact of life in schools, including the general perception by many of our teachers that they are free agents hired to teach a subject to students. This perception is reinforced by placing a teacher in a classroom with students and shutting the door. Who knows what goes on in there?

During the past 40 years, the public has insisted on knowing what schools teach and what students are learning. Education is expensive to operate, about 9,000 dollars per student each year in 2008, and the curriculum is value-laden. Schooling is an important business—too important to be random or accidental. The planned curriculum tells the public and all educators what is intended. Testing, in many instances, tells us what students may have learned because they studied the curriculum. The connection between this intention and the outcome is the plan for learning. It would seem obvious that this document, the curriculum, should be understood by all people in a school.

Curriculum mapping presents an operational picture of what is actually taught; it is reporting, not planning. Once we have the map of the curriculum as it is experienced, we can begin to make adjustments and improvements to align the *curriculum planned* and the *curriculum experienced*. Remember, curriculum work in schools is the process of achieving the goals we have established for our program and our students (Jacobs, 2004; Udelhofen, 2005).

Both "plain" mapping and "fancy" mapping are found in schools. Plain mapping might be a simple process of having each teacher reconstruct what he or she teaches each grading period or each month of the year. Fancy curriculum mapping might use computer software such as Curriculum Mapper, Rubicon Atlas, or Eclipse that, in some cases, even matches state standards to the curriculum reported.

In my experience, just having teachers reconstruct their own classes on large sheets of paper and taping these sheets to a wall for all to see will suffice to identify many common problems. Content gaps and redundancy between grades will emerge immediately. So will skills and content that are taught in multiple locations such as metrics (i.e., math, science, physical education, home economics, and social studies). Some teachers may even experience difficulty in trying to reconstruct what they taught over the course of a year. Some will want to just use the issued textbook to build their reconstruction.

What happens during this process is that your staff will discover that they really aren't teaching a curriculum (the planned set of learning experiences). Rather, they will see that they are teaching unrelated subject matter and not always in any logical order. Is there any connection between this subject matter being taught and the goals for this curriculum?

Even those teachers who would use the textbook to represent their teaching map would find that many districts use several different text series by different publishers, so coordination and sequencing are difficult (Figure 6.1). There are very few school districts that can afford to buy subject textbooks for all grades K–12 at the same time. A more common pattern found in schools is that there will be one or two publishers in each subject by level (elementary, intermediate, secondary). These publishers, of course, do not coordinate their texts.

Kindergarten	First Grade
Weather and seasons	Animals and pets
Interrelationship of plants and animals	Farm animals
The sun, our principal source of energy	Zoo and circus animals
Classification of living things	Common birds
Simple measurement	Where plants live
How plants are alike and different	Where animals live
Farm animals	Grouping and classification
Care of pets	Air and water
Observing animals	Sun, moon, stars
Indoor plants	Seasons and weather
Earth, moon, and stars	Fire and temperature
Sounds	Simple measurement

Figure 6.1 A curriculum with multiple publishers, K–1 science

Curriculum mapping provides an authentic picture of what curriculum is really being taught. The power of this process is in the explicitness of the map. It provides us with the big picture before we begin to work on coordinating the parts.

At the most basic level, curriculum mapping will fine tune the scope and sequence of the school studies. *Scope* refers to the boundaries of the curriculum (i.e., what's included) and sequence is the order or arrangement of the curriculum. In the traditional sense, the curriculum can be envisioned as a grid of grades and subjects:

	Reading	Math	Science	Social Studies	Art	Music
Grade 1						
Grade 2			THE CURRICULUM			
Grade 3						

Once the curriculum is laid out or mapped, expect to see more definition in the elementary and secondary grades than in the middle grades. Because the achievement by students is so disparate in grades 5–9 (i.e., this is where there is the widest range of achievement), and because students are so preoccupied with their own development during this period, many schools simply choose to repeat elementary subject matter during these years. This relearning procedure is wasteful, of course, and results in there not being a solid conception of the curriculum in the middle years. Faculty in intermediate schools should be asked to identify large goal areas that can anchor subject matter in various courses. Asked another way, what should be in the curriculum, and what should be targeted during these years to link the elementary and secondary curriculums together? Working backwards, the faculty might ask what knowledge, skills, and attitudes are prerequisite to being a successful high school student?

Usually, the curriculum is mapped using some predictable organizers: by content, by skills, and sometimes by all state standards targeted for that grade or level. It is important to the process of mapping, however, that there also be a column marked "concepts" or "big organizers." As the curriculum is streamlined and reformed through curriculum mapping efforts, a rationale for changing (i.e., the criteria) will be needed. During the mapping process, teachers may find some content in subject areas that can't be justified or doesn't seem to fit anywhere. Why, for example, do we teach the names of all state capitals in the United States in social studies? What is this knowledge used for? A basic curriculum mapping form would look like this:

Subject: Science			4th Grade	First 9 Weeks
Concepts	I	Content	Skills	State Standards
	I	I	I	I
	I	I	I	I
	I	I	I	I

A few caveats are in order concerning the curriculum mapping process. First, although most teachers recognize the value of planning in curriculum work, few teachers like to be inspected. The curriculum leader should identify a small group of lead teachers who can guide the faculty through the curriculum mapping process. It is the author's experience that resistance to the process will be less if near peers lead the group process.

Second, and directly related to the suggestion above, it is important to let teachers know that the curriculum maps will not be used in teacher evaluation. There will be a great variety in quality and detail in the initial mapping efforts. Teachers should not be compared for their efforts, and the leadership group may find it necessary to encourage small groups of knowledgeable teachers to polish some of the less complete maps the first time around.

Finally, mapping should be introduced as a recurring process that will be used to check the efficacy of the curriculum improvement efforts from time to time. Realigning the curriculum and adding and subtracting from its volume should be the actual on-going curriculum work in your school.

ALIGNMENT CRITERIA

There are a number of factors that will assist in aligning the curriculum in that they provide an ordering process to increase logic and effectiveness in what is taught in the classroom (see Figure 6.2). The first of these is the element of time. Time is the most precious resource in all curriculum activity. Students spend approximately 15,000 hours in the classroom during their 12 years of schooling, and this time must be used wisely. The value of the content to be taught, in terms of time, must be assessed and reflected in the maps created by teachers. Asking teachers to prioritize content may be confusing at first, and the concept of a "minimum curriculum" (i.e., need to know) and a maximum curriculum (i.e., nice to know) may be helpful. Discussions about the merits of curriculum parts will pay large dividends when curriculum improvement efforts begin.

Surprisingly, state standards and standardized testing results will not be very helpful in such an alignment. Most standards are minimal or structural in nature, and they are not tied to values identified by teachers and the school community. The school-level discussions about the worth of items in the curriculum will define how teachers treat the content in their classrooms. Do we want the students to have a conceptual understanding of this information (i.e., the big picture), or is this particular content of the curriculum foundational to all subsequent learning (i.e., detailed knowledge)? Instructional designs (e.g., interdisciplinary, core, spiral, etc.) result from these discussions about the value of subject content (McNeil & Wiles, 1990).

Time can be estimated using units such as weeks or even 6- or 9-week grading periods. In the eighth grade math, what is supposed to happen in the first 9 weeks? The second 9 weeks? Many readers will recall how the absence of such a time orientation resulted in never covering modern times in their history classes. Such a time orientation will help teachers see that some learning may be more important than others, in terms of the large goals previously established.

Type	Purpose	Activity
Critical–Creative Thinking	Construction of new knowledge and forms	Model-building, free imagination
Problem Solving	Issues analysis, skills application	Current events, futurism
Cooperative Learning	Social skill development, shared decision making	Cooperative activity, group work
Interdisciplinary	Connecting information	Organizing, ordering
Conceptual Learning	Understanding	Big ideas, familiarity
Inquiry Approach	Awareness, interest	Stories, unknowns
Skill-based Instruction	Manipulation, patterns	Rules, practice, ordering
Content-based Instruction	Knowledge acquisitions	Facts, representative form

Figure 6.2 Eight common curriculum designs

A second criterion for aligning the curriculum is the assumptions made about how much learning should occur. Learning can be quite detailed and sequential, or it can be more global and use representative knowledge. For example, if a freshman English class is studying American authors by reading a series of books, what is the intention of the curriculum? Do we want them to know that Stephen Crane wrote the *Red Badge of Courage* and be able to reconstruct the story, or are we using authors to represent periods of time, a writing style, or historical events of importance?

Instructional designs can be content-based or conceptual. We can present knowledge to students in a planned sequence or in a repeating thematic pattern (i.e., a spiral curriculum). We can expect students to recall what is taught or to apply it in terms of their own experience. These assumptions about learning will greatly influence how we align the curriculum found on our maps. Hopefully, the clear goals established for the curriculum will make our intentions clear to everyone participating in this process.

A final criterion for aligning the curriculum may be the idea of prerequisites or curricular dependence. In Math, for example, can we teach higher-level concepts without the foundational operations (i.e., addition, subtraction, multiplication, and division)? Can we teach middle school world history without elementary geography? As the faculty inquires into these relationships, the interdependence of the subjects may become clearer. We are planning a K–12 set of coordinated experiences!

1. State standards and testing schedules

2. How the content contributes to larger goals

3. Time requirements

4. The focus, broad or narrow

5. Any prerequisites

Figure 6.3 Alignment criteria

As the reader is discovering, curriculum development work can be pretty complex. Like an architect designing a home, the curriculum leader is putting together a design for learning that will accomplish a set of desired objectives using real school resources. The assessment of such a curriculum can only be made in terms of the stated intentions. The result of experiencing the curriculum, the student learning experience, is totally dependent on the quality of the curriculum planning.

STANDARDS IN THE CURRICULUM

During the period from 1990 to the present, a major change occurred in what is studied and tested in schools. Today, 48 of the 50 states and the District of Columbia have instituted some kind of testing program in schools, and many of those same states have adopted a standards-based curriculum. In some districts, the term *curriculum* has regressed from a set of planned "common experiences" to a simple set of uniform standards to be mastered while the student is in school. Even more disturbing to curriculum specialists is that approximately one-half of all teachers in our schools today were certified during this era and believe that such a narrow curriculum is both normal and desirable.

The standards movement has, of course, helped to define and focus instruction. It has also made the measurement of student achievement much easier for school districts. On the other hand, such an artificial force in schools has diminished the value of some subjects, and skewed teaching toward only those subjects that are being tested. An unbalanced curriculum has resulted in many school districts, and the act of curriculum development has become increasingly mechanical rather than dynamic. We have been going backwards in our quest to service the needs of all students in school.

Whether the reader is enthusiastic about curriculum standards or feels they severely limit curriculum designs, it is a fact that these standards are the dominant feature in most schools today. Standards must, therefore, be included in the detailed instructional planning for school improvement. Standards can contribute to the structure of curriculum maps, frameworks, and scope and sequence charts. They can help teachers target Grade Level Equivalents (GLEs). In addition, standards can contribute to any internal discussions at the school level about the value of certain subject areas.

Aligning the school curriculum with state-mandated standards does not mean that these two things are the same. Standards may provide a definition of the minimum curriculum demanded by the tax-paying public. Standards may also contribute a general definition of what must be taught. Rarely, however, do state-mandated standards contribute to the why-and-how discussions that define classroom delivery of the curriculum. Issues such as relevance of material, developmental appropriateness for students, contribution to achievement, and adaptability to the future needs of students remain open to discussion and interpretation. This discussion is the business of the school faculty.

At the classroom level, teachers will need assistance in aligning the various instructional components (e.g., tests, texts, review materials), pacing student learning, meeting grade-level expectations, and addressing student motivation. Most important, the curriculum leadership at the school must work diligently to disassemble the notion that standards are the curriculum. Standards are, at best, a contributing factor in defining the overall curriculum for a school or district. They may tell us what the curriculum is, but they certainly don't tell us why or how to teach the standard. Discussions with faculty about the meaning of intellectual competence, the transfer of knowledge, and the reality of multiple intelligences can contribute to this uncoupling of standards from the general curriculum improvement process.

AN EMERGING BLUEPRINT FOR SCHOOL IMPROVEMENT

With the conclusion of the mapping and alignment process, the school is poised to begin promoting positive changes in curriculum. Among the tools available are committees that promote solid communication with the school community and building leaders, data from internal needs assessments, goal statements with subobjectives, and a factual map of what is actually transpiring in the classrooms (see Figure 6.4). As the analysis stage of the curriculum cycle draws to a close, a blueprint for school improvement emerges. This blueprint has scale, priorities, and definition and allows faculty to compare the vision for improvement with current practice. Discrepancies between what is intended and actual practice are now perfectly clear.

1. Good communication with school community

2. Data from needs assessments

3. Curriculum maps

4. Discussions of alignment

5. Use of standards and grade-level equivalents

Figure 6.4 Components of detailed curriculum planning

In the next stage of the curriculum development cycle, the design stage, the curriculum team will address needs comprehensively and redraw school practices for greater effectiveness. The curriculum leader will use a number of tools available in all schools to steer the curriculum improvement effort toward its desired conditions. The process of curriculum improvement has become active.

PLANNING TOOLS THAT EMPOWER

Regardless of the school or the district, all leadership roles have basic tasks that must be completed for general functioning. Leaders must set and prioritize goals and put into place standards and policies. The curriculum leader needs to establish long-range planning and appropriate organizational structures. He or she must secure resources and appoint competent personnel. Facilities must be dedicated to certain types of instruction and funding secured to fully operate programs. Human relations and communication paths need promotion, and a way of evaluating performance agreed upon. All of these things, of course, are related (see Figure 6.5).

For the new curriculum leader, it is important to recognize that tasks such as those listed above reflect leadership style and the general way of working in the school. These everyday tasks present the curriculum leader with a way of steering or encouraging certain patterns of behavior. For this reason, I call these key planning tools *curriculum steering devices.* They represent opportunities for the leader to encourage certain behavioral patterns:

Budgets: It is obvious that budgets are important because money is the equivalent of fuel for promoting change. Most curriculum work is like a distance-rate-time problem in math. The more money that is applied (rate), the faster work gets done. The less money available, the longer the change takes to complete. Money and budgets serve to prioritize projects, and the curriculum leader often has the power to support changes using budget priorities as a vehicle.

1. Budgets

2. Committee assignments

3. Public relations

4. Use of technology

5. Allocation of resources

6. Curriculum design activities

7. Staff training opportunities

8. Formatting curriculum documents

9. Writing reports of progress

10. Evaluating and validating progress

Figure 6.5 Ten tools that empower curriculum leaders

Committee memberships: Most curriculum work in schools is done by committees that seek to find consensus for change. The dynamics of such group interaction are immensely important to the success of any project. The curriculum leader has the power to create and compose such groups by assignment. Sometimes such group assignments can also be used to minimize the influence of disruptive members.

Public relations: An area of power overlooked by many curriculum leaders is public relations and various publicity efforts. These opportunities represent a communication "offense" by forming opinion and building consensus for change. School leaders don't have to be idle in waiting to be noticed—they can promote change by disseminating information. The news media seeks stories about education and will follow most stories suggested by the curriculum leader once a relationship has been established.

Technology utilization: The power of technology is recognized by all in the 21st century, but schools still do not use this resource as an effective communication tool. With 95 percent of all homes having a telephone and nearly 75 percent of homes with school children having a computer with e-mail capacity, reaching and informing the public about school change should not be difficult. Web pages, blogs, electronic committees, computer surveys, reports on line, and a host of other techniques enlarge the power of the curriculum leader to communicate and influence.

Resource allocation: Resources available for curriculum work are often expandable. Curriculum leaders may rewrite grants, reallocate or combine existing resources, solicit long-range fiscal commitments, and use other similar means of placing priority on certain types of school improvement. Sending a teacher to a conference for additional training, for example, shows commitment to the reason for such training. The curriculum leader makes such decisions each day and, in doing so, exhibits the power to quietly promote change.

Curriculum design work: More than other steering devices the very act of designing curriculum is empowering. As noted earlier, curriculum represents values, and the program experienced by school children, by its very design, shows preference for some values over others. Indirectly, and sometimes even directly, the curriculum leader guides the selection and adaptation of values in developing school programs.

Staff training: Most curriculum development is totally dependent on teacher classroom skills for implementation. The difference between the novice first year teacher and the veteran teacher is more than time in service. In-service teacher training (i.e., staff development) adds skills and knowledge to the basics of teaching gained in college coursework. Curriculum leaders can "build" a teacher through the selection of training the teacher experiences. Programs in schools can be enhanced by carefully selecting training experiences that foster the skills needed to implement the curriculum.

Document formatting: Often overlooked by curriculum leaders is the power of documents to legitimize activity and sway opinion. In a presentation to a school board, for example, a pie graph may say more than a ten-page paper on the topic. Educators live in a world of too much information, and to be able to "write the headlines" by selecting the document format is a powerful tool.

Report writing: Something that has always interested me is how little attention educators pay to history. Go into any school and ask what has happened during the past decade and you'll receive a blank stare. Yet, previous history in schools can be used to rationalize change. Like all historical documents, the writer of educational reports has the power to project patterns from all existing information. The many periodic reports written during the development of a curriculum project establish the history of the event forever.

Evaluation: Finally, possessing the power to assess and evaluate programs, people, and processes represents a very strong steering lever for curriculum work. Evaluation designs tell us "how to count," and enable the same information to be presented in a certain way for a certain purpose. With student achievement, for example, comparing the progress of a class in third grade and then again in fourth grade makes for an assessment of achievement gain. On the other hand, comparing fourth grade achievement year to year as most state achievement reports do may present a very different and false pattern of student achievement in a school.

These ten curriculum steering devices represent planning tools that empower the curriculum leader. Unlike administrative leaders who have line authority to operate and maintain the school, the curriculum leader (who is on the staff rather than in the administration) gains his or her power from promoting positive changes in the school program. Without a single order or command, the curriculum leader can be powerful at what is most important: improving student learning.

SUMMARY

Detailed planning is necessary for successful curriculum development. Without a nuts-and-bolts look at what is actually happening in the classrooms of a school, curriculum and instruction are not connected.

Curriculum mapping and curriculum alignment are techniques to gain an accurate picture of what is actually being taught in classrooms. The mapping process, at a minimum, should include content and skills, concepts, and any instructional standards mandated by state testing. Gaps in the curriculum, or redundancy in the curriculum, can easily be spotted by all teachers using this format.

Curriculum alignment rearranges the curriculum by priorities. Time, the value of subject matter, and dependence of some learning on others are all criteria for "moving the curriculum around." Traditionally, the middle grades (5–9) will be the least organized area of any school district curriculum.

Finally, in detailed curriculum work, the curriculum leader has some tools that provide power for changing. The budget, committee memberships, public relations, uses of technology, resource allocation, curriculum design work, staff training, document formatting, writing reports, and evaluating programs all present ways to promote desired change in schools. The "working power" of curriculum leaders is quite unlike the traditional line authority of a building administrator.

Sample Problem and Leader Actions

Exceptional Education: Inclusion

Activity	Actions
Curriculum work designing programs for special or exceptional students are governed primarily by law. One of the most challenging tasks for curriculum specialists in recent years has been to design the educational experiences in regular classrooms to meet the requirements of full inclusion. Laws governing such programs are federal, and they are based on the assumption that all students will have greater success in academics and social development if they are not separated from their peers on the basis of disabilities.	**Review various laws including 93-380, 94-142, and Individuals with Disabilities Education Act.** (Resource A—R21)
While there have been federal laws governing programs for exceptional students for more than 50 years, two laws have dominated the development of school programs; 94-142 (1972) and IDEA (1990). The first law, 94-142, was defined by the "least restrictive environment" (LRE) clause, which held that exceptional or special students should be placed in regular classrooms if possible. Numerous definitions of exceptional were provided by this law, and most categories of disability were eligible to be "mainstreamed" into regular classes.	**Read the law carefully. Many educators think that this law still governs all exceptional student programs.**
A second powerful federal law, Individuals with Disabilities Education Act (IDEA) was passed in 1990 after research showed little difference in performance for students in special classrooms. IDEA was characterized by the concept of *inclusion,* which held that all students were to be placed in regular classrooms unless there were compelling reasons against such a placement. In the mainstream model, students with disabilities "qualified" for regular placement, whereas in the inclusionary classroom all students were initially placed with regular teachers unless they displayed a dysfunction.	**Determine how this distinction will have influence on the regular classroom curriculum.**
The task for curriculum leaders, then and now, is to somehow accommodate the twin concepts of *equity* and *excellence.* Most classroom teachers, until recently, were not trained to work with special students and, in fact, both the National Education Association and the American Federation of Teachers have opposed inclusion policies.	**Determine what legal or contractual issues are at stake here. Establish a teacher-led committee to study.**

(Continued)

(Continued)

Activity	Actions
These powerful teacher groups can exert enormous pressure on schools and districts, but they are not as powerful as the law of the land.	
The curriculum worker in a school will have about 14 percent of all students with exceptional designations; the vast majority being either emotionally disturbed or having selected learning disabilities (SLD). Under IDEA, former special teachers will be distributed throughout the school either as a team-teacher (collaboration model) or as a consulting teacher (collaborative consultation model) or as simply co-teachers with common responsibilities (co-teach model). The school can create any model it desires to service all student needs, including special needs, but with few exceptions they cannot place students in isolation or exclusionary classrooms.	**Determine how teachers** will **accommodate students with special needs in the classroom.** (Resource A—R22) **Learn about training that may be needed for regular teachers.** (Resource A—R17)
In reality, this curriculum work is about law and money. An initial step for the curriculum leader is to study the above-cited laws and contact those associations (Resource B) that focus their attention on these students. Visits to other schools and districts will help round out a general understanding of what is required.	**Build a resource list of agencies. Search Internet for model programs in your area.**
New ways of teaching may be required. What kind of accommodations would have to be made for blind students? For the hyperactive student, or the highly gifted student (also a special designation under 94-142)? For the most part, the curriculum work will consist of modifying the existing program and teaching strategies to incorporate all the diversity.	**Construct a map of the curriculum and design examples of changes in the instruction.**
Curriculum leaders will have to also consider the rights of the nonexceptional student and the concept of academic excellence. How much compensation and accommodation can occur until the planned course of study is mired in exceptionality procedures? How much of the normal instructional resource base should be dedicated to specialness?	**Review instruction budget for possible modifications.**
The curriculum development process will consist of efforts to come into compliance with what is called for in IDEA (1990). The process should be gradual, not abrupt, and there will be a heavy need for teacher training. Issues such as student progress reporting will have to be confronted, and technology may find application in many of the special cases involving students who don't learn easily in large group settings.	**Use developmental staging to visualize gradual change.**
As in previous cases, any changes planned should be timed with both expenditures and outcomes identified in advance. Validation of changes should be a public process, and board involvement may be required in situations in which political activity cannot be contained by rational procedures.	**Seek time with your superiors to share the kind of change that must occur.**

END NOTES

Jacobs, H. (2004). *Getting results with curriculum mapping.* Alexandria, VA: Association for Supervision and Curriculum Development.

McNeil, J., & Wiles, J. (1990). *The essentials of teaching.* New York: Macmillan.

Udelhofen, S. (2005). *Keys to curriculum mapping.* Thousand Oaks, CA: Corwin Press.

Curriculum Improvement Means Staff Development

Curriculum improvement in schools, ultimately, calls for staff training. The difference between what is currently being done, and what is desired, is totally dependent on classroom teachers for implementation. Staff development, sometimes called in-service training, connects curriculum and instruction.

All curriculum work in schools is directed toward improving teaching. We provide teachers with an orientation, better instructional tools, new knowledge and skills, or a better classroom facility so that they can be more effective in teaching the students. It is vital that curriculum leaders connect to staff development efforts in the school or district and help define teacher training in terms of curriculum improvement.

TEACHERS AS THE CRITICAL INGREDIENT

When classroom teachers are assigned to a room full of students to teach a subject, they will be only as effective as the organization that surrounds them and the training they have had. A noisy workplace, insufficient materials, a nebulous curriculum, and many other factors can sabotage good teaching. But even when all of these prerequisites are satisfactory, a teacher can fail to be effective because he or she doesn't understand the curriculum plan or possess the skills to implement the curriculum.

A good example of this was an attempt, several years ago, to implement cooperative learning in classrooms in the United States. Cooperative learning was a fairly simple concept using group learning and classroom management techniques to activate learning. However, many teachers were baffled by a concept that used mixed-ability groups (rather than like-ability grouping), allowed greater student participation, and required close classroom supervision and management by the teacher. Elementary teachers were fairly skillful at such small-group management, but secondary teachers had not been taught this set of skills. Ultimately, the concept, so promising for achievement, waned in many middle and high schools.

When curriculum designers set up a new program with new organization, materials, assessment, and teaching behaviors, they must include staff training in the design and implementation phases. Unless teachers in the classroom can do what is called for by the curriculum design, the plan is doomed to fail. It is as simple, and as complex, as that.

In Figure 7.1, the relationship between staff development and curriculum work is shown as an activity that leads to a unit of study for students. Following development of the plan, which includes a teacher guide for implementation, the teachers receive training through an in-service program. Armed with this training, the activity is field-tested under controlled conditions before being disseminated into all classrooms. Often, such training reveals gaps in teacher preparation for delivering the curriculum. The use of new technologies in many schools provides a common example of an area in which many teachers are characterized by such deficiency.

WHY MANY TEACHERS DISLIKE STAFF DEVELOPMENT

There are many reasons why teachers have a low opinion of the in-service training they receive, the most frequently cited being the irrelevance of the experience. For many teachers, there is little or no connection between the scheduled staff development experiences and what they do in the classroom each day. Although this is surprising to many new curriculum leaders, it shouldn't be. Most classroom teachers do not have the comprehensive perspective of training held by those persons in leadership roles. Further, it is often true that the selection of in-service opportunities for teachers is not made with school improvement in mind. Too many workshops

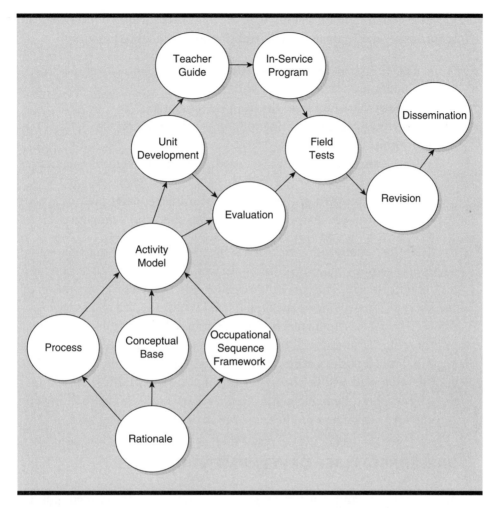

Figure 7.1 Staff development as an extension of curriculum work

are scheduled because of the availability of a resource. In particular, the use of National Board Certified teachers and representatives of publishing companies to "fill" in-service days is distressing.

Not providing a rationale for a staff development experience for teachers is like a classroom teacher starting a lecture to students without an introduction to that lecture. Under such conditions, students in the classroom are forced to guess what the teacher is speaking about, and quickly tire of the game. Likewise, teachers sent to staff development experiences without an explanation of why often arrive with a set of negative attitudes that minimize the effectiveness of the training (Wiles & Bondi, 2004). Repeat the offense several times and the attitude hardens: staff development is a waste of time!

In addition to not knowing why they are being trained, teachers also report general unhappiness with training experiences because

- The trainer is an outsider with no knowledge of local classroom conditions.
- The teachers have had the training previously.
- The timing of the training interferes with more pressing classroom events.
- The trainer appears disorganized or unknowledgeable about the subject.
- The environment or timing of the training is unsatisfactory.
- The experience does not respect the teachers' personal time.

There are many other reasons why teachers might not appreciate in-service training, but any of the above would be a legitimate reason for a lack of enthusiasm. The curriculum leader can, of course, overcome all of the above by the way he or she designs and structures the in-service experience. Above all, helping teachers understand why they are being trained and how such training will improve classroom instruction is one way to begin to build a positive attitude toward training. It is highly unlikely that staff development will be successful without answering these basic questions for teachers. Remember, the implementation of any curriculum plan is completely dependent on the cooperation of classroom teachers.

PREFERRED STAFF DEVELOPMENT DESIGNS

There are many staff development designs, using a variety of mediums, to share information about the curriculum with teachers. Some of these designs are more effective in bringing about real change than others. Generally speaking, research has found that any teacher-to-teacher pattern is superior to other, less personal approaches. Teachers learn best

1. Teachers training teachers.

2. Train a small group of teachers as a team.

3. Train for specific skills only.

4. Training to complete desired profile.

Figure 7.2 The most effective training patterns

from teachers who are like them but who are slightly different in what they know. The literature calls this relationship *near peers* (Rogers, 2003).

Near peers are people like you, but perhaps having slightly different experience. If you were going to buy an automobile, for example, you'd want to speak with someone who already owned that same kind of car. They would be like you (a car owner) but different (because they've already bought the car). Teachers share many likenesses, but their own teaching experiences are often different.

One time-tested staff development design is called *teachers training teachers*. In this design, a teacher is trained somewhere and then returns to his or her school to train other teachers. Classroom teachers trust this source because the trainer teaches in a room in the same school that they do. This is a particularly effective design for learning a skill—using a sort of demonstration or "show and tell " approach.

A second successful design is to train a team or other grouping of teachers together. As they learn, they give each other assistance and feedback. Once back in the school building, they all have that similar training experience to build on. This model is particularly effective in overcoming a reluctant participant.

A third best bet is a sort of training-by-objectives model in which certain knowledge or skill is required to operationalize a curriculum. If, for example, teachers were asked to operate a new software program for geography class, the teachers would be certified by training to complete the task. Such a design is very easy to rationalize to teachers: We need this skill to operate the program.

A final winning teacher training strategy is to provide a profile of the teacher needed in a school program and then let individual teachers select the skills they need the most to be like that profile. As the individual teachers profile themselves, they come to understand that they are better at some things than others. Conversely, other teachers in the building might have strengths and weaknesses in other areas. If the curriculum leader can match up those teachers needing training with building teachers who are skillful, then staff development becomes a natural sharing of teaching skills.

What has been learned to be ineffective in staff development is to bring in an outside consultant (even a teacher), who knows little about the culture of the school, and let that stranger tell the faculty what they should be doing (Sarason, 1971).

Figure 7.3 presents a summary of research about factors that increase the odds that teachers will accept an outside innovation or professional development training.

Higher Risk ←			→ _Lower Risk_	
Source of Innovation	Superimposed from outside	Outside agent brought in	Developed internally with aid	External idea modified	Locally conceived, developed, implemented
Impact of Innovation	Challenges sacrosanct beliefs	Calls for major value shifts	Requires substantial change	Modifies existing values or programs	Does not substantially alter existing values, beliefs, or programs
Official Support	Official leaders actively oppose	Officials on record as opposing	Officials uncommitted	Officials voice support of change	Enthusiastically supported by the official leaders
Planning of Innovation	Completely external	Most planning external	Planning processes balanced	Most of planning done locally	All planning for change done on local site
Means of Adoption	By superiors	By local leaders	By representative activities	By most of the teachers	By group consensus
History of Change	History of failures	No accurate records	Some success with innovation	A history of successful innovations	Known as school where things regularly succeed
Possibility of Revision	No turning back	Final evaluation before committee	Periodic evaluations	Possible to abandon at conclusion	Possible to abort the effort at any time
Role of Teachers	Largely bypassed	Minor role	Regular role in implementation	Heavy role in implementation	Primary actor in the classroom effort
Teacher Expectation	Fatalistic	Feel little chance	Willing to give a try	Confident of success	Wildly enthusiastic about chance of success
Workload Measure	Substantially increase	Heavier but rewarding	Slightly increased	Unchanged	Workload lessened by innovation
Threat Measure	Definitely threatens some clients	Probably threatening to some	Mild threat	Very remote threat to some	Does not threaten security of autonomy
Community Factor	Hostile to innovations	Suspicious and uninformed	Indifferent	Ready for change	Wholeheartedly supports the school

Figure 7.3 Factors influencing the reception of change

ASSESSING STAFF DEVELOPMENT EFFORTS

Training for teachers can be conceptualized as consisting of three basic levels. The first level is what is considered basic for all teachers in a district. When teachers are hired, for instance, it is desirable that they have been through an accredited four-year teacher education program at a university because such programs have certain requirements that have been verified. In recent years, many states have endorsed short-run training programs at the intermediate and secondary levels. Such programs may fill a gap, but they are largely ineffective in promoting stable quality education in schools. But even after hiring fully certified teachers, it is likely that the school or district will provide orientation training to new recruits to familiarize them with specific district programs and procedures.

At the second level of training, each school building represents a unique design for learning. All schools have different kinds of students attending and different local environments. The curriculum at a school has usually been adapted to the needs of the student population and the aspirations of the school community. Schools also often have special learning programs and special equipment. Schools give teachers additional on-the-site training to prepare them to work in that specific program.

Finally, each individual teacher has personal strengths and weaknesses. Some have vast experience with children, whereas others don't. Some will know how to handle technology whereas others will be reluctant. Some teachers will work naturally with other teachers and parents whereas others may exhibit isolationist tendencies. At the third level of training, every teacher will need to be assessed and supported while they acquire new or compensating skills and knowledge to be effective at their school (Castetter, 2000).

When assessing staff development efforts in a school, we can focus on the plan itself, the programs and training experiences that make up the plan, the effect of the staff development on the participants, or how the training affects the curriculum. Most curriculum leaders will construct an evaluation model using these four lenses to assess their teacher-training program (Figure 7.4).

1. How does this staff development contribute to the curriculum plan?

2. Are the training programs appropriate for implementing the plan?

3. What effect does the training have on the participants?

4. How do we expect this training to impact the curriculum?

Figure 7.4 Evaluating staff development programs

1. What is the purpose of our staff development?

2. How does this staff development plan serve our curriculum?

3. What do our teachers say they need?

4. Does the plan comply with district and state requirements?

Figure 7.5 Key questions about staff development

The staff development plan will be shaped by available resources, obvious needs suggested by various assessments, valued teacher input, and state and district requirements. Figure 7.5 shows the key questions for the curriculum leader to ask.

The various workshops and training experiences offered within a staff development program should possess themes, and these themes should serve to organize all activities. The curriculum leader should resist planning a workshop because of the availability of a visiting consultant or because a vendor offers to lead a workshop free of charge. Such experiences are guaranteed to raise the "why" questions from teachers and, ultimately, to build resentment by teachers for wasting their time.

The effect on the participants, usually teachers, can be measured with workshop evaluations and by participation patterns. My experience is that teachers will stick with any training they perceive as useful. It is a good practice to disseminate teacher evaluations quickly once they are compiled. Curriculum leaders can count on the fact that teachers will share opinions with each other about the training, with or without such summaries.

Finally, and most important, curriculum leaders can administer an assessment showing how the training affects the curriculum. Measures of awareness, usage, student achievement, and teacher desire for further training all can serve as yardsticks for evaluation. The program should improve the degree to which teachers are prepared, and such preparation can easily be quantified and shared with others.

A WORD ABOUT ADULT LEARNERS

Adult learners differ in a number of significant ways from school children and even college students in how they approach training. Planning training activities for classroom teachers will demand sensitivity to these differences (Knowles, 1973). See Figure 7.6 for a list of these differences.

1. Adults base learning on previous knowledge and experience.

2. Adults like adult-to-adult communication rather than teacher–student talk.

3. Adults, because of their experience, require more time to process input.

4. Adults like to be able to share what they already know about subjects.

5. Adults have many events competing for their time and attention.

6. Adults always want to know the utility of the information.

7. Adults have learning handicaps and different motivators.

8. Adults can be anxiety-prone, and they sometimes fear failure or loss of self-esteem.

Figure 7.6 Key questions about staff development

As we grow, we experience and we learn. By the time we are adults, most of us have established patterns of thinking and a base of knowledge that serves as our reality. Unlike school children, who often are nearly a blank slate, the adult learner will usually place new information in one of their established knowledge files. If the new knowledge doesn't "fit," it usually will be rejected. In rare cases, mental files will be adjusted to accommodate new information on old topics.

Adults, and especially classroom teachers, do not want to be a student again. Teachers prefer to be an adult who learns from another adult in adult ways. This alone makes lecture a poor method for all school staff development.

The curriculum leader will find that teachers may take longer to digest information than the leader is used to. Unlike the school-age learner or even the college student, adults have a vast reservoir of information from life experience. As the teacher absorbs, weighs, and assesses staff training, it may take longer for a thoughtful response or question. This sifting process is important, and leaders should allow time for such reflection in training sessions.

Because teachers are used to teaching, they will naturally want to share what they already know about any topic in a staff development session. Rather than attempt to suppress such public input, the staff development leader should always schedule for questions, observations, and discussion.

Teachers at workshops may sometimes be preoccupied with other things. It is natural for them to be thinking about classroom responsibilities, home concerns, or even mundane things they must do that day after the training. These are real concerns and should not be seen as inattentiveness or disrespect. Anyone working in a school knows how hectic each day can be for the classroom teacher.

Planners of staff development for teachers should count on early audience questions about the relevance of any training. The first question for any person in a training experience is "What is the value of this new knowledge?" Come prepared with an answer for this question.

All persons have learning handicaps, and they can be quite pronounced in some adults. Listening, for example, can often be selective in a world of too much noise. Understanding what motivates adults can also be difficult. Some teachers love to learn, whereas others may be hoping to meet some other need by attending the training session. The leader should accept both of these cases as a possible source of motivation.

Finally, adults fear failure, humiliation, or any other act that might attack their self-esteem. In asking questions of an audience, the curriculum leader must provide outlets for free expression or for just remaining quiet.

CURRICULUM AS THE RATIONALE FOR STAFF DEVELOPMENT

Curriculum planning defines what students will experience in the classrooms. Such planning also tells school leaders what teachers must know, or be able to do, in order to activate such plans in their own classroom. Staff development is the direct connection between curriculum and instruction.

If the reader can see instruction as a subset of curriculum, and staff development as a subset of instruction, then teacher training always exists to implement the curriculum in the classroom. Even teacher training for personal enrichment can be used to enlarge the background of the teacher so that they can make more instructional references and connections for students.

In some schools, there is no apparent connection between classroom teaching, workshops, and the curriculum design provided to teachers. Such schools, without intentions, guidance, or preparation, are rarely effective in working with students.

SUMMARY

Teachers are the critical ingredient in learning. Implementing curriculum plans at the classroom level depends entirely on teachers. Staff development connects curriculum and instruction in the school.

Many teachers dislike in-service training when they can't see the connection to the classroom, feel their time is being wasted, or are being trained by persons who don't know their needs.

The best training, according to research, is teacher-to-teacher models in which someone with a like background introduces a near peer to something new. Patterns such as teachers training teachers, team training, training by program objectives, and individual growth models all work for teachers.

Staff training can be assessed by its design, by evaluation of individual workshops and experiences, by the effect on individual teachers, and by how such training affects the program in the classroom.

Curriculum development serves as the only true basis for assessing staff training in schools. Schools that don't make the connection between curriculum and classroom instruction and staff development programs rarely have success in teaching students.

Sample Problem and Leader Actions

Staff Development: Training Plans

Activity	Actions
Education in the United States does not invest heavily in training when compared with other institutions in business, medicine, and the military. In some school districts, training of staff is perceived as a luxury.	**Write a statement to share connecting training, teaching, and student learning.** (Resource A—R1)
Staff development is difficult to plan because of the different needs of teachers and the less-than-clear connection between curriculum and instruction.	**Determine how the needs of a teacher with 1, 5, and 20 years would differ. Construct a career plan for any teacher.**
The logic of the staff development plan will be important to gaining teacher involvement and motivation. What is the overall design of such training at your school?	**Conduct a needs assessment of existing training and the training desired by teachers. What is common?** (Resource A—R10)
The conditions under which staff development is delivered will influence its effectiveness. Special attention must be given to how teachers perceive these conditions.	**Check to see what the teacher contract says about when and how training is to occur.**
Research suggests that the most effective training is teacher-to-teacher. When outsiders are employed, they are rarely credible or seen as knowledgeable about local conditions.	**Select a training model from those featuring teachers training teachers.**
Teachers are most concerned about the element of time. They often perceive training opportunities as competing for time they need for another activity.	**Develop a master training schedule at your school. Tie events to curriculum changes.**

END NOTES

Castetter, W. (2000). *The human resource function in educational administration.* Upper Saddle River, NJ: Prentice Hall.

Knowles, M. (1973). *The adult learner: A neglected species.* Houston: Gulf Publishing.

Parkay, F., & Stanford, B. *Becoming a teacher: Breaking the mold.* New York: McGraw-Hill.

Rogers, E. (2003). *Diffusion of innovations* (5th ed.). New York: Free Press.

Sarason, S. (1971). *The culture of the school and the problem of change.* Boston: Allyn & Bacon.

Wiles, J., & Bondi, J. (2004). *Supervision: A guide to practice* (6th ed.). Upper Saddle River, NJ: Prentice Hall.

Closing the Circle Through Evaluation

For 30 years, the enormous cost of education has driven an accountability movement in the United States. What began as a funding crisis in the 1980s has given rise to a perspective on schooling. Very few people in curriculum doubt that this preoccupation with standards and testing is a permanent fixture in planning school programs. I believe that this condition should be acknowledged and seen as an asset rather than a workload factor. Evaluation can serve as a powerful tool for making things happen.

GENERAL FUNCTIONS

Evaluation has at least four general functions that interface with curriculum work in schools:

- making explicit the philosophy and the rationale for instructional design,
- collecting data for making judgments about program effectiveness,
- making general decisions on a day-to-day basis, and
- rationalizing changes that are proposed and implemented.

This book has addressed the role of philosophy on many levels. As I have noted, philosophic statements are used to convey purpose. Such statements also reveal the values that support all school programs. In addition, philosophy defines the curriculum by noting the scale of responsibility.

At the classroom level, philosophy guides instructional design by providing a rule of thumb for choosing approaches, materials, and methodology. The intended purpose of the curriculum design ultimately determines what the teacher is to do each day.

Evaluation can also serve to structure the ways in which we measure our success or failure in teaching students. If a program has broad and flexible conceptual goals, it is likely that the data used to measure such a program will also be general in nature. If the program is narrowly focused, then highly specific data might be used to show results.

Said in a different way, the evaluation design and progress of data collection will, ultimately, define the curriculum. This is especially true in an age of high-stakes testing when the curriculum is often skewed by the desire to do well on the tests.

On a more practical level, the evaluation process established by any school will contribute to decision making and even structure discussions about curriculum. In earlier chapters, I noted that philosophy can be abstract and that the use of numbers can bring such abstraction into focus. As the evaluation design establishes desired outcomes, faculty will begin to discuss success and failure by such numerical measurements (e.g., "We are still below the upper quartile, what do we need to change?").

Finally, as has been discussed in the planning chapters, evaluation designs can help gain commitment from superiors by identifying exactly what will happen after change has occurred. This notion of return-on-investment is popular with board members who feel compelled to enforce accountability for taxpayer dollars.

As the curriculum plan stretches out over several years, it is the data gathered for evaluation that provide continuity. Teacher membership in a school turns over at a rate of 10 percent a year, principals change about every four years, and board members usually serve about three years. If a curriculum project is 36 months in its implementation, the curriculum leader will be talking to a different audience than when the project began. Evaluation will provide the historical trace of successes and failures.

A GENERIC DESIGN

Establishing an evaluation design in a school is fairly simple. The most difficult part of this process is to convince others that measurement is important. Such an understanding will follow seeing the curriculum as a design for learning.

The six steps to establishing an evaluation plan for your school include structuring, collecting data, organizing data, analyzing, reporting findings to others, and activating data.

Structure the evaluation

Collect the data

Organize the data

Analyze the data

Report the data

Activate the data

Figure 8.1 Generic evaluation design

Structure

The structure of the evaluation design follows the philosophy and curriculum design of the school. More specifically, the criteria used to make decisions (i.e., values) will define whether the evaluation is to be broad or narrow. Are we measuring only academic progress, or are we concerned with the total growth of the student? As the curriculum leader reaches decision points about the scale of the curriculum, these decision points can be used for organizing the evaluation design.

Collection

The collection of data occurs in those areas where curriculum decisions are made or anticipated. Most schools, for instance, would collect standardized test data. Many schools might go further and look at internal grading patterns and promotion records as well.

If the goals for the curriculum are broader, the school might also collect and organize data such as attendance and participation in school activities. Still broader would be various attitudinal assessments by students, teachers, and parents. If the curriculum is concerned with the application of knowledge, portfolios of student projects might be archived.

For most curriculum development activities, the data collected are proof that the intentions of the change are being met. Such data may be displayed in a graph or timeline showing the baseline (i.e., beginning) and a record of change and improvement over time.

Organization

To be effective, all the data collected must be in the same format and stored in a uniform way so that it can be retrieved easily. A storage and retrieval system will need to be established that allows access to the data in a form that is useful. The curriculum leader will need to work closely with the data manager in the school office to design the system.

Analysis

Data analysis is conducted according to a schedule established by the evaluation design. Some indication of the data sample (i.e., how much will be examined) should be agreed on in advance of analysis. Are we looking for a trend, or are we proving that we met a target?

The analysis should be carried out by as many people as possible because the entire process of evaluation is really a communication device about how well the school is doing in accomplishing its curriculum goals. Funding the analysis should be an item in the curriculum budget.

Reporting

Reporting the findings of the evaluation review is a vital part of the process. The author advocates widespread dissemination of findings as a matter of basic integrity. If the findings are positive, we should congratulate ourselves. If the findings are less than we expected, then we have just rationalized further change.

The curriculum leader should give extensive thought to the reporting medium. Although formal written reports are good for superiors, the "real" audience might be the community, which pays for schools and is vitally interested in the results of educating the students. Evaluation reports are reinforcing to the values held by those in the community. The Internet provides instant access to anyone interested in evaluative results.

Activation

Evaluation tells us how we are doing. In the traditional curriculum cycle of analyze, design, implement, and evaluate, the evaluation portion closes the circle. Evaluation will indicate where we are and what we need to look at next; it returns us to a new analysis of the school program.

THE PURPOSE OF EVALUATION

Evaluation is useful in tightening up the instructional program at the school, and within that general purpose there are four areas of focus: Program design, process, product, and personnel. Evaluation questions can be formulated so that the evaluation will gather data on these four areas, and the evaluation can be constructed in such a way so as to shed light on a particular area.

When the goal of evaluation is to tighten and improve the school program, the first focus is to examine the concept, looking at the overall structure of the finished curriculum. Evaluation procedures should validate goals and purposes set out by planners in the analysis stage. The critical question of this focal point is, "Do we have the kind of program we intended?"

A second focus of the evaluation is to examine processes or how the curriculum is being operated. This evaluation might consist of checklists to determine the efficiency of system parts such as communication, finance, and planning procedures. The key question asked would be, "Are we efficient in delivering these services?"

A third focus of the program evaluation is the actual product of the curriculum. Using tests, surveys, and structured feedback, we seek to measure what has been accomplished. A key question might be, "Are we getting the desired outcomes?"

The final focus is on the personnel and their role in the curriculum. Using observation and interviews, we would seek to determine roles and effective participation. A critical question might be, "Are our personnel making a direct contribution to the program as planned?"

These questions establish the structure of any school program evaluation.

Is this the program our planners intended?

Is this program efficient in its delivery?

Is the program delivering the desired outcomes?

Are the personnel making a direct contribution to the program as planned?

Figure 8.2 Four evaluation questions

EIGHT AREAS FOR STUDY

Although there are many areas that could be studied in any school curriculum, eight areas can be identified that would provide a base of feedback for program planning. Those eight areas are the program design, facilities usage, policies and regulations, resource utilization, student performance, teacher effectiveness, staff development, and parent–community feedback (Figure 8.3). Each of these areas is defined by a series of evaluative questions:

Program Design

Facilities Usage

Policies and Regulations

Resource Utilization

Student Performance

Teacher Effectiveness

Staff Development

Parent–Community Feedback

Figure 8.3 Eight areas for study

Program Design

1. Is the program concept consistent with the overall philosophy of the district leaders?

2. Does the program articulate (i.e., fit) well with other levels of schooling?

3. Are dedicated resources for this program equal to other programs?

4. Does this program have internal consistency in the form of goals and objectives?

Facilities Usage

1. Do the location and allocation of spaces for this program reflect its priority?

2. Are learning spaces organized in a manner consistent with the instructional intention?

3. Has teacher input been used in designing the facility or spaces?

Policies and Regulation

1. Are any new policies necessary to allow this program to fully function?

2. Do any policies or regulations contradict the spirit of this program?

3. Is there an established way to address policy changes in development of this program?

Resource Utilization

1. Can this program be funded according to the objectives of this program?

2. Are there funds earmarked for innovation and further change in this program?

3. Is there an established procedure for assessing future resource needs and planning for their acquisition?

Student Performance

1. Is student evaluation in this program systematic and continuous?

2. Do teachers recognize student performance as a measure of success?

3. Are parents involved in the evaluation of students and the program?

4. Does student evaluation give direction and indicate where improvement is needed?

Teacher Effectiveness

1. Can teachers suggest ways to improve this program?

2. Is teacher evaluation tied directly to program improvement?

3. Have teacher talents and contributions been fully explored in this program?

4. Are there any unplanned administrative constraints on teachers in this program?

Staff Development

1. Are monies budgeted for teacher training and tied to the goals of the program?

2. Do teachers have an opportunity to define their staff development program?

3. Can we show that staff development is, in fact, improving this program?

Parent–Community Feedback

1. Are members of the community involved in the formation and maintenance of this program?

2. Are members of the community kept informed about changes to this program?

3. Is there an effective communication vehicle for receiving community input about this program (Wiles, 2005)?

USING TECHNOLOGY IN EVALUATION

The many new interactive technologies of the 21st century allow curriculum leaders to streamline evaluation efforts at the school level. Test data, state and district records, student reporting, and many other assessment sources are available on-line in digital format. Analysis of these records, including reconfiguration of the data for special purposes, is now an option (Association for Supervision and Curriculum Development, 2008; Western Michigan University, 2008).

The use of new technologies goes much further than securing, analyzing, and disseminating reports. Formats for planning and evaluating, such as PERT/CPM, are available on the Internet. (See: portal.acm .org/citation.cfm?id=1217043). These tools often come with tutorials and even assisting consultants at no charge. Many schools post their evaluation models on-line for other schools to see.

Because the number of home computers with Internet access has grown dramatically in the past 10 years, surveys can be conducted with near-instant feedback from teachers, parents, and community.

Curriculum leaders can use graphics on most computer programs to enhance reports and provide simple summaries of their messages.

The possibilities for collaboration in-district and beyond the district are global in their scope. Networks of schools are a reality today. These networks connect teachers and administrators across districts for many purposes.

New technologies are available to assess teacher performance and deliver corrective staff development programs, at school or at home. Teachers can also retrieve research and various examples of successful school programs elsewhere through professional associations like the Association for Supervision and Curriculum Development.

Entire curriculum programs are on-line, and there are live Web cams of teachers teaching in a variety of subjects.

Finally, software to keep track of the many frontiers of school evaluation and to keep records in many areas is available on-line and free. The new curriculum leader need only type in a key search word and access the resource (Planwell, 2008; Project Kickstart, 2008).

SUMMARY

Evaluation is an important part of the curriculum development process. Curriculum leaders analyze their condition, design curricula, use implementation strategies, and then evaluate the entire process for results. The difference between the planned curriculum and the achieved curriculum leads to a new analysis stage.

Evaluation in schools serves at least four functions: to clarify and make explicit the philosophy or values in the curriculum, to collect data for making judgments, to guide the decision-making process on a daily basis, and to rationalize proposed changes to the curriculum.

A generic procedure for evaluation would be to first structure the evaluation, then collect information, organize such data, analyze the data, report the findings, and apply the data. Eight areas are common in establishing a curriculum design: program design, facilities usage, policies and regulations, teacher effectiveness, resource utilization, student performance, staff development, and parent–community feedback.

Technology can be useful in monitoring and managing a complex school evaluation design. In particular, curriculum leaders will find the Internet to be a resource of great value.

Sample Problem and Leader Actions

Evaluation: Establishing a Design

Activity	Actions
A preliminary evaluation design should be set up as soon as possible tying curriculum and outcomes together in an if–then relationship.	**Identify what data can be retrieved from conventional sources at your school.**
Evaluation should be perceived as a series of proofs that answer questions or document accomplishments.	**Develop a list of questions you would want answered about a school curriculum.**
Data for evaluation should be readily available to teachers, parents, and the widespread access to this community-at-large.	**What medium will best allow widespread access to this data?**
The assessment of evaluation data should take place according to a predetermined process.	**Design a flow chart showing how to retrieve such data.**
Curriculum decisions are made on the basis of the best available data. From such data, a hypothesis about outcomes can be generated	**Determine who at your school would review data and make the decisions about future curriculum development.**
An evaluation design will emerge with data drawn from eight areas.	**Find out which of these areas are most important when you establish this system.**
Technology can be used to mechanize data gathering and retrieval.	**Figure out which technologies are currently available at your school.**
The development of the evaluation program will be gradual and orderly.	**Use a developmental staging process to outline how this program will unfold.**

END NOTES

Association for Supervision and Curriculum Development. (2008). Retrieved May 15, 2008, from http://www.ascd.org/

Planwell. (2008). Free planning software available from www.planwell.org

Project Kickstart. (2008). Free planning software available from www.project kickstart.com/

Western Michigan University. (2008). Evaluation tools available from The Evaluation Center, 4405 Ellsworth Hall, Western Michigan University, Kalamazoo, MI 49008-5237.

Wiles, J. (2005). *Curriculum essentials: A resource for educators* (2nd ed.). Boston: Allyn & Bacon.

Coordinating Successful Curriculum Work

The many steps of everyday curriculum work require detailed coordination. Without such detail, efforts to improve learning experiences for students spin away into abstraction or evaporate quite rapidly. It has been said that the half-life of any innovation in education is two years: That is, the innovation becomes 50% diluted every two years. In this chapter, I present the concept of comprehensive planning as a means of avoiding this evaporation effect.

Comprehensive planning, stated simply, is a systemic look at all that is occurring in any change effort. Sometimes, despite the best intentions of the leader, nothing happens at the classroom level. Systems approaches seek to manage or control the many variables that interact in school change and constrain activity toward preferred ends. The curriculum leader must see each piece of the effort in terms of how it contributes to the targets for school improvement. For example, why are we offering a particular workshop to teachers? What do we expect to happen because the teachers have attended this workshop?

SOME REASONS FOR CURRICULUM FAILURE

If we look at a standard curriculum development cycle (analyze, design, implement, evaluate), we can see many of the reasons curriculum work is not successful:

Analyze

1. There is no real plan and the effort can't be assessed.

2. Leaders fear a true analysis because it might reveal weaknesses.

3. The analysis never gets beyond jargon and slogans.

4. Leaders actually enhance the assessment because they feel it is necessary.

Design

1. The design is unachievable because of special conditions.

2. The design challenges bedrock values of those who must implement it.

3. The design is couched in vague or misleading terms.

4. The design is ungrounded and "blue sky" or is a "bandwagon" thing in which everyone is joining, without thoughtful consideration.

Implement

1. The primary supporters of the design (superintendent, board) change.

2. The change process is simply too complex to be fully understood.

3. The time frame for changing is too short or unrealistic.

4. Training is not provided to carry out the changes desired.

Evaluate

1. No baseline data to accurately measure progress are established.

2. Evaluation is not in a useful or understandable format.

3. The source of evaluation is not generally trusted.

4. No one is fully responsible for assessing the process (Wiles & Bondi, 2007).

From the few reasons for failure cited above, and there are many others, the reader can see the reason for comprehensive planning. A comprehensive plan provides a deductive logic beginning with the purpose of the curriculum and where we wish to go. It breaks down the parts so the effort does not seem so overwhelming. It provides evidence, from day one, that movement is occurring. Finally, the comprehensive plan serves to put all interested persons in communication with each other. Whether at school, a district, or at the state level, curriculum work is rarely successful without a detailed and comprehensive plan.

THE ELEMENTS OF A COMPREHENSIVE PLAN

The traditional model for curriculum development (see Figure 9.1) shows a progression from big picture to small details. Data are used to prove existing conditions and measure progress. Goals become the large program organizers, and objectives and standards define the general program. Once clear, the process promotes specific activities to implement the plan. Finally, the progression from the curriculum intended to the curriculum experienced in the classroom is measured or validated by evidence acceptable to all.

The process of developing a school curriculum is analogous to constructing a house. At first the shell (floors, walls, and roof) emerges, followed by framing out specific rooms. Each room is then given detail, and finally the finishing appointments are provided. In the same way, a curriculum plan begins with blocking out large goals and defining those areas with specific objectives, which then become programs, subject areas, maps, and instructional plans.

The most important thing for a new curriculum leader to understand is that the implementing activities do *not* come before the design of the plan. Certainly some variables, such as school buildings, might not be able to wait for a detailed plan to be developed. But items such as teacher training, the procurement of instructional resources, and buying technology for the teacher should be defined by a theme and set of clear instructional goals. Surprisingly, in some schools and districts, many of the implementing variables (equipment, materials, staff training, finance) are provided independent of the ongoing curriculum development process. If the means are allowed to define the ends, curriculum leadership will appear superfluous and accidental, and natural teacher follower-ship will be nearly impossible. What the comprehensive plan should do is provide a logical and comprehensive road map for everyone.

WE'RE ALL IN THIS TOGETHER

In the most successful schools and districts, there is a general feeling of being a team that exists to serve students. Curriculum work is basically a

Philosophy > Program Concept > Broad Goals >

Objectives > Program Design > Evaluation Standards >

Needs Assessment > Curriculum Alignment > Program Design >

Course Frameworks > Lesson Planning > Instruction

Figure 9.1 A traditional model for curriculum development

problem-solving process that helps students learn, and the school is the most cohesive organizational unit for such effective program development. As the leader of that school effort, the individual in charge of curriculum must convey to others that they—the school community—are all in this together.

The questions that will be on the minds of teachers are fairly obvious and are defined in terms of their own work. Teachers need to know what to expect from the expenditure of their energy, and they will want to know how the many pieces fit together. Parents, of course, will have more specific concerns about how the curriculum affects their children. This is natural and a source of motivation to participate in school improvement.

The curriculum plan defines the boundaries of all activity. The curriculum leader must signal the staff and parents that the administration supports the effort, that resources are available, that the time commitment is defined, and that this is ultimately about children in classrooms. Once the curriculum leader communicates these facts, the entire school community will embrace proposed changes.

PLANNING TOOLS

To communicate with others, the curriculum leader must understand communication itself. Communication among individuals in organizations is a delicate art requiring, among other things, self-discipline and a cooperative spirit. The spoken language, particularly English, is full of subtleties, and superimposed on the actual words are a host of nonverbal cues that can alter the very meaning of speech. Written communication, while not spontaneous, is far more stable. Even more precise, for curriculum work, are various pictorial communications.

The most basic visuals used in planning and implementing programs include data summaries and checklists. Data summaries can provide massive amounts of information in a simple format (see Figure 9.2). Teachers and parents will rarely have the time to wade through large data sources, and such summaries can make convincing arguments for both the existing status of a program and projected outcomes.

Checklists can also be particularly useful in validating progress in curriculum work (see Figure 9.3). This is especially true when using a "yes or no" format.

Graphics, graphs, and charts are also great vehicles for communicating quickly with others about proposed or existing conditions. Graphs, such as a pie graph, are particularly effective in communicating progress to school boards and the public. Flow charts are valuable for showing how one activity transitions to the next. A simple graphic, such as the one shown in Figure 9.4 to define the concept of *interdisciplinary*, can be worth a thousand words.

School	Age of School	Assigned Capacity of the Building	# of Students	# Student Transfers	% New Teachers	% Staff Attendance	Ratio White-Black-Hispanic Students	% Limited English	% Free and Reduced Lunch	% Student Mobility	% Student Attendance	Suspensions 1986–1987	Corporal Punishment 1986–1987	Student Not Promoted Over No. Grades	Student Dropout Year	# Compensatory Education Students
Lake Stevens	1975	1292	1088	312	14	96.8	8/59/33	2.5	48.5	36	90.7	268	4	11.2/3	4.1	247
Palm Springs	1957	1222	1169	0	0	97.1	8/1/91	10.4	17.5	36	92.1	269	0	23.7/4	6.0	125
Charles Drew	1967	1220	876	35	14.6	97.1	0/99/1	0	53.9	42	90.2	118	71	21.0/2	10.8	266
Madison	1955	1007	841	31	10.9	96.9	3/73/24	5.7	48.3	39	91.6	84	8	35.3/3	9.1	197
Citrus Grove	1924	1417	1358	154	9.4	96.5	4/9/87	17.9	55.2	38	91.9	233	0	15.3/3	6.9	321
Citrus Ridge	1969	1120	1107	189	5.1	96.7	26/39/32	2.8	25.0	28	92.7	157	0	1.8/3	5.7	74
Mays	1951	1050	733	300	13.5	94.8	10/54/35	4.1	68.3	41	90.0	158	0	24.3/3	4.5	114
Redlands	1926	1290	1281	1155	8.1	97.7	58/16/24	1.5	27.6	31	91.4	354	1	20.0/3	5.8	131
Campbell Drive	1976	1516	1266	721	8.5	96.8	20/28/51	2.1	50.3	37	86.3	373	0	18.3/3	5.2	168
Filer	1956	1355	1372	146	9.4	96.7	3/10/86	9.5	51.0	28	92.6	50	1	4.7/3	9.1	237
Nautilus	1949	1243	1327	999	12.5	97.0	22/18/59	10.8	48.5	40	90.0	267	0	17.1/2	14.6	265
Norland	1960	1348	1377	360	4.5	96.6	19/67/13	0.9	25.1	25	95.5	170	99	8.7/3	1.3	161
Shenandoah	1926	1436	727	8	3.0	96.4	4/2/94	17.9	55.2	34	91.9	99	0	11.8/2	10.3	138

Figure 9.2 Data summaries quickly convey critical information

Program Descriptions	Status		
	Yes	No	Action Plan to Achieve
Microcomputers, either permanently located in all classrooms or on mobile carts, are available for classroom use.			
Additional mobile computers will be available to move into classrooms when necessary or to develop a mini-lab when desired.			
Each school will have at least two qualified full-time computer education teachers.			
Each school will have at least two complete computer labs containing a minimum of 16 microcomputers and have a ratio of two students per computer. Each lab will include necessary computer system hardware, software, and peripheral equipment to meet current and future trends and developments. The complete computer labs will consist of necessary space, lighting, seating, air cooling system, electrical system, and security, plus access to telecommunications.			
Daily lab schedules should include time set aside for independent student use.			
All students in Grades 6 and 7 will be scheduled into one of the computer labs for a minimum of three hours a week in order to meet the state requirements for computer literacy.			
A minimum of two computers with needed peripherals will be located in the teachers' work area for teacher use (i.e., grading, software review, word processing, etc.).			

Figure 9.3 Checklists are used to show work completed

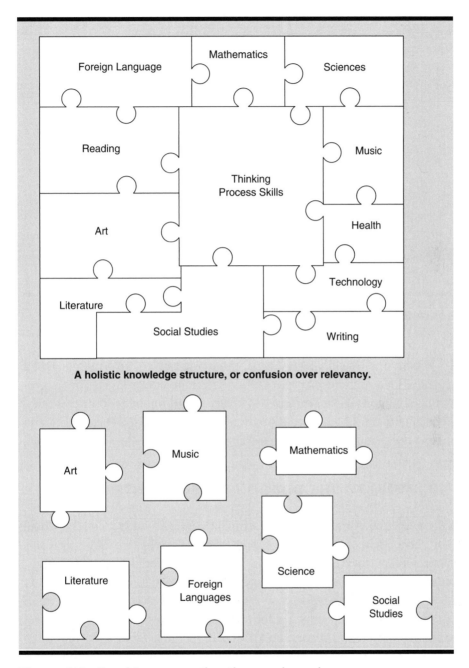

A holistic knowledge structure, or confusion over relevancy.

Figure 9.4 Graphics are worth a thousand words

Timelines are of special interest to anyone participating in a long-term curriculum project. Gantt Charts, a time bar indicating duration, show how various components of change line up over time. A simple time and activity grid like the one in Figure 9.5 can present multiple activities in an understandable manner.

Activity	Time	Responsibility
School Curriculum Team Monthly Meeting	February 24	Assistant Principal for Curriculum (APC)
Vision Visits to Schools	March 1, 8, 15	Team Leaders
Quarterly Evaluation report	April 15	APC
State Testing Dates	April 22–25	Principal/Counselors
Parent Feedback Group	May 2	School Community Leaders
Final Summer Staff Development Plan Due	May 15	APC/District Staff Development
Summer In-service (Teachers)	June 20–28	Team Leaders

Figure 9.5   Activity, time, and responsibility

Finally, there will always be a great interest in any money being expended for a curriculum project. Budgets are indicative of priorities in promoting change and can be likened to fuel in an automobile. Without money, projects "run out of gas" and ultimately fail. Tying budgets to activities and making these budgets public helps everyone see how the project will unfold.

REPORTING TO THE BOARD AND SUPERINTENDENT

It is my experience that regularly informing the superintendent and the school board about school-based projects pays dividends, whether they solicit this information or not. These reports can be formal, delivered at board meetings, or informational, on a need-to-know basis using small papers delivered at intervals. Each of these reports can legitimize any project by creating a written record of what is happening. As the summaries grow in number, the project becomes more substantial and builds its own rationale for further support by the school leaders. In contrast, many school projects in curriculum have died from a lack of support from above because the school or district leaders did not know what was happening. Such confusion is simply unnecessary.

The curriculum leader must attempt to be succinct in reporting to school or district officers. School board members, for example, usually get a large stack of papers to study the week before each board meeting. In reality, many board members can only read the summaries of these papers because of time limitations. Any report to board members should simply summarize the most important aspects of the project. Simple visuals, like the pie graph, are particularly valuable in conveying meaning quickly.

TIMING IS EVERYTHING
IN SCHOOL IMPROVEMENT

Like all institutions, schools have a culture that determines how they work. One of the most distinctive things about school cultures is that they operate one year at a time. School begins in late summer or early fall and concludes in late spring or early summer. The next fall, another year begins. Most schools and districts do not think in terms of five- or ten-year increments, and this is very important information for school planning.

The curriculum leader should use natural time breaks in planning, such as holidays (Halloween, Thanksgiving, Christmas, spring break) or six- or nine-week grading periods. Where will we be by Thanksgiving? What are our goals by the time the spring holidays come around? Teachers think this way about school time, and using these markers will make planning easier for all.

Another important thing about time in schools is how the planning process ties into the budgeting process. School boards generally develop district budgets based on the actions of state legislatures, who complete their budgets for education in late spring. The board in each district projects a budget for buildings, teachers, materials, and so forth around February or March of each year. For a curriculum project to get into the district budget, the board needs the full information shortly after Christmas. School-level needs for budget are developed in November and December. All of this means that the curriculum leader must be preparing to ask for funds for the next fall nearly one year in advance.

The best budget strategy for any curriculum project is to tie it to existing goals at the school and district level rather than to any new goals. Projects tied to new goals will only be considered after existing goals and needs have been satisfied. Because school boards don't know what legislatures will do about school budgets, projects not tied to existing programs and goals will be perceived as add-on items and will be the first to go if budgets are smaller than expected.

One last piece of information about curriculum projects and budgets that is important to understand is that schools and districts spend their money in conservative ways. Most superintendents and principals fear running out of money late in the year. This is especially true if there is a history in your state of being asked to return money because of a fiscal shortfall. Understanding this pattern of boom-and-bust expenditure is important because schools are often overly cautious and have too much money in February and March. Because the following year's budget is usually based on what has been spent in the current year, schools and districts will expend resources very rapidly in mid-spring. These funds are often called "sweep-up" money because they are swept together hurriedly. The curriculum leader who is ready with a "wish list," tied to a major planned curriculum project, may well pick up a lot of funding under these conditions. The organized school will have a better argument for this money than one that can't tie requests to on-going projects.

PROGRAM EVALUATION AND REVIEW

The comprehensive plan in curriculum work provides a kind of bird's eye view of all activity. The school community will know what you are trying to do, your strategies and activities to implement the plan, the people responsible for each part, and how they will pay for this plan. Most important, the school community and citizens-at-large will know what to expect as a result of this project having been funded.

Business leaders today sometimes use a technique developed by the United States Navy called *program evaluation and review technique,* or simply PERT. This technique looks at a project comprehensively and assesses its progress according to something called the *critical path method* or CPM. Stated simply, in a project some things are critical and some things can wait until later. When we look at the many activities needed to activate a curriculum project, the dependency among the parts is what defines the critical path. For example, staff training is often essential for activating a new curriculum design and must occur before a program is started. Instructional materials needed in the fall should be budgeted for in the early spring and ordered before the current school year ends.

The project planning process consists of the following parts:

1. Setting the start date.

2. Setting the completion date.

3. Determining the scope of the project.

4. Envisioning the project in phases.

5. Identifying milestones or other observable products.

6. Listing tasks by project phase and in the order to be accomplished.

7. Estimating personnel needed to accomplish each task.

8. Determining whether training is necessary to accomplish each task.

9. Ordering or identifying dependencies among tasks.

10. Predetermining review points.

11. Projecting cost estimation.

12. Providing a cost–benefit analysis.

Although the above list seems challenging, the simple truth is that these are essential questions about the project. What is the scale of this work? How will it be performed? What will it cost? Will the effort be worth doing in terms of what is achieved?

PERT/CPM charts depict task, duration, and dependency information. Each task is connected to a successor task. As the curriculum leader looks at all of the events and activities in a plan, the dependence of one step on another becomes obvious and defines the critical path to be followed. Simple time estimates for these critical events will define the length of the entire project. Nonessential activities can be scheduled around these essential events and activities (see Figure 9.6).

A BATHTUB FILLING UP

For teachers, parents, and other members of the school community, all of these considerations will not be in focus. Each person will want to consider their assignment as an isolate, asking how they will personally be affected by the changes. Providing all persons with a road map that clearly communicates how the many pieces fit will prove invaluable for attaining buy-in (Modell, 1996).

Equally valuable will be a review and reporting procedure that projects what is to happen and measures what did happen. The accountability factor of this review and reporting is the key to its effectiveness. Being able to project to leaders the who, what, when, and how much, and then summarizing what was accomplished each reporting period, will ensure success for the program. As referenced above, such order and logic will also aid the project in getting a lion's share of any sweep-up funds when it is time to spend out the budget.

Teachers in particular will feel really good knowing that their most valued commodity, time, is not wasted. They will watch the "bathtub filling up" with pride like any winning team does. Such feedback, numerical in nature and summarized by planning tools, will promote motivation.

1. Be aware of and plot all necessary activities to implement plan.

2. Identify and link together activities that are dependent (one before another).

3. Estimate the time required for just those dependent activities.

4. The sum total of time required for the dependent activities is the "critical path."

Figure 9.6 The PERT/CPM perspective

BOOSTERS THAT CAN ACCELERATE CHANGE IN SCHOOLS

Curriculum leaders can experiment with various activities and rewards that may boost or accelerate change in schools. Schools are notoriously "flat" in their use of titles and rank, and most schools have few resources to reward teachers for their work. Sending a group of teachers to another district or to a conference to view something new is usually well received by individuals who rarely get to leave their classrooms. Providing mini-grants to a teacher or group of teachers may also boost morale.

It is my experience, however, that simple recognition of the work teachers are doing can be a tremendous motivator. Taking a page from industry and letting the individual or group of teachers "own" part of a curriculum project pays dividends. Just like an autoworker who certifies that their part of the car is well made, teachers can be allowed the freedom to exhibit creativity in building a new curriculum. Being recognized for work in developing school programs is a special payoff for teachers and may bring the "genie out of the bottle."

SUMMARY

Comprehensive planning is critical to successful curriculum work in schools. Sharing information about the many parts of any change project will unite faculty and promote feelings of togetherness.

Curriculum leaders can use planning tools to increase communication among members of the school community. Speaking with charts, graphs, visual summaries, and other tools will prove superior to written or spoken feedback. Communicating with superiors, the superintendent and the board, with reports will increase the stability of the project.

Timing of change is an often overlooked element in planning. In particular, funding of curriculum projects is based on timing of requests for money. To the organized school leader, picking up "sweep-up" money will prove simple. Using review and evaluation methodology (PERT/CPM) will allow others to follow the logic of planned change and to justify its expense in terms of outcomes.

Finally, comprehensive plans lead to pride of accomplishment. Faculty and school community will see progress, like a bathtub filling up, as time progresses. Such positive feedback will increase participant motivation. Small boosters, particularly recognition for ownership of certain activities, will accelerate change in schools.

Sample Problem and Leader Actions

Comprehensive Planning: The Final

Activity	Actions
You are a new curriculum leader at Little Guys Elementary School. The school houses 600 students including 85 exceptional students (14%). Your school population earns 52 teaching units by state formula.	**Determine how exceptional student education (ESE) will affect decision making.** (Resource A—R12)
Because of Federal Inclusion law, most of these "special" students will be in regular classrooms.	**Decide how you might deploy your ESE teachers and best use space to benefit the curriculum.**
Your building was constructed in 1988 and has an administrative suite, two specialty rooms, a library, and 24 classrooms with two wings of 12 rooms. There are five portable classrooms on the campus.	**Determine how you might deploy your teachers and use this space to the benefit of the curriculum.** (Resource A—R22)
Your school has a SIT (School Improvement Team) with six parents and five teachers. The group has not changed for three years.	**Decide how you would like to use this group and whether you should elect new members.**
The school is configured in a 1–3, 4–5 grade pattern, reflecting a human development rationale.	**Look into whether this is the optimum pattern for an elementary school curriculum.**

Activity	Actions
Little Guys school has not done well on state and is rated as a "C" school. Forty-five percent of your students are receiving free lunch, which reflects a low socioeconomic population.	**Research whether there is a connection between low socioeconomics and student achievement.**
The district is going to give LGE 30 computers this fall. Would you place them in a lab, give them to classroom teachers, or put them in strategic places throughout the school.	**Determine how these computers might make your curriculum more powerful.**
Five of your teachers have requested your permission to create a new curriculum using only Web-based resources.	**Research how granting permission for this will affect the regular curriculum. What can you expect if you deny this request?**
Your faculty at Little Guys is very experienced, with an average of 14 years in the classroom. What kind of staff development do you envision for these teachers?	**Determine whether it matters that your staff is older.** (Resource A—R17)
As you walk the halls, you notice that the janitors have placed all student classroom chairs in rows. You wonder if this is how the teachers want them arranged?	**Decide whether you should speak to the janitors or whether your teachers should take care of this.**
You will be meeting with your teachers tomorrow for the first time. What are the most important items you should discuss relating to the curriculum?	**Develop an agenda for this one-hour talk.**

END NOTES

Modell, M. (1996). *A professional's guide to systems analysis* (2nd ed.). New York: McGraw-Hill.

Wiles, J., & Bondi, J. (2007). *Curriculum development: A guide to practice* (7th ed.). Upper Saddle River, NJ: Prentice Hall.

Resource A

Reproducible Planning Sheets

R1—Curriculum Report Checklist	
<u>Statement of Purpose</u>—Describes the specific problem or need addressed by this change	____
<u>Philosophical Position</u>—Identifies beliefs that undergird this approach	____
<u>Supporting Documentation</u>—Statistics, research, and other authoritative documents to support	____
<u>Critical Elements</u>—Major program areas to be addressed	____
<u>Program and Learning Objectives</u>—What is to be accomplished in each area above?	____
<u>Observable Standards</u>—What will be seen by anyone viewing the project in the future?	____
<u>Facility Needs</u>—What physical resources are needed to succeed?	____
<u>Equipment and Communication Needs</u>—What tools are necessary for success?	____
<u>Material and Transportation Needs</u>—What structural curriculum support is necessary?	____
<u>Areas to be Assessed During Design Phase</u>	____
<u>Timeline for Implementation</u>—Is the timeline with staging complete?	____
<u>Budgetary Needs</u>—Includes categories and estimates	____
<u>Evaluation and Validation Checkpoints</u>—Review points and criteria	____
<u>Task and Responsibility Graph</u>—Identifies what, who, when	____
<u>Simple PERT/CPM</u>—Shows the order and dependence of major items	____
<u>Dissemination Plan</u>—Displays way of sharing this information	____

R2—Facility Standards

The facility standards for our school fit the curriculum design and instructional pattern established by the School Curriculum Team (SCT). Our facilities should allow for varied instructional experiences, support our curriculum concept, and meet the needs of all personnel at the school.

1. Essential Considerations
   - Increased attractiveness by use of color scheme and graphics.
   - Adequate instructional spaces and equipment for each program.
   - Clustered grade level classrooms.
   - Flexible classroom spaces.
   - Access to Internet throughout the building.
   - Adequate storage areas for student learning materials.
   - Twenty percent re-usable spaces in building.
   - Acoustical treatment in all movement areas.

2. Desired Considerations
   - Laptop computer for each teacher 24 hours a day.
   - Outdoor classrooms on campus.
   - Exceptional education conference spaces.

R3—12 Suggestions for Effective Meetings

1. Involve participants in planning the meeting _____

2. Acknowledge the schedule of others _____

3. Provide ample lead time for the meeting _____

4. Leave a portion of the time unscheduled _____

5. Make spaces ready and presentable for the meeting _____

6. Provide food or snacks _____

7. Divide meeting into 15-minute segments and move on _____

8. Keep discussions short and to the point _____

9. Acknowledge legitimate dissention _____

10. Invite participant feedback, and use it _____

11. Follow meeting with memo or e-mail summary _____

12. Don't forget to test all media before the meeting _____

R4—Curriculum Management Outline

Needs Assessment

School   _____

Community   _____

Philosophy and Goals

Determined by entire school community   _____

Based on needs of students   _____

Curriculum

Based on needs assessment and philosophy   _____

Includes defined sequence of content concepts and skills   _____

Provides for all learners   _____

Includes checklists for measuring progress   _____

Is articulated with other levels of schooling   _____

Instruction

Includes management system to ensure implementation   _____

Has grading system that reflects the curriculum   _____

Appropriate materials support   _____

Provides for continuous student progress   _____

Organization

Uses arrangement that support curriculum intent   _____

Allows best deployment of teaching skills   _____

Is cost effective for return on investment   _____

Staff

All teachers qualified to participate   _____

Teacher responsibilities clearly delineated   _____

Provides for systematic in-service   _____

Systematic evaluation of teachers and administrators   _____

R-5—School Data Sheet

Enrollment   _____

Average daily attendance   _____

Absences per teacher per month   _____

Percentage of low socioeconomic backgrounds   _____

Number of Exceptional student education (ESE)
students (excluding gifted)   _____

Number of gifted students   _____

Student mobility in—out   _____

Number of students with disciplinary referrals   _____

Number of students expelled or suspended during year   _____

Dropouts (eighth grade and up)   _____

Percentage of students receiving D's or F's in classes   _____

Achievement percentile by grades on standardized tests   _____

Number of parent volunteers   _____

R6—Student Information Sheet

Student name _____

- address_____

- phone_____

- e-mail_____

I live with: Father and mother _____   Father only ____   Mother only____

                Stepfather ____   Stepmother ____   Both ____

                Grandparents _____   Other _____

Father's name _____   Occupation _____

Mother's name _____   Occupation _____

Names of brothers and sisters

_____

_____

_____

Date of birth:_____

I was born in: City_____   State_____

(Continued)

(Continued)

Do you wear glasses when reading?   Yes_____   No_____

Can you see writing at the front from a seat in the back?   Yes_____   No_____

Do you have difficulty hearing from the back of the room?   Yes_____   No_____

How much time do you spend on homework each night?_____

My favorite subject is_____

The subject I like the least is_____

My hobbies are_____

After school I like to_____

When I finish school I want to_____

_____

R7—Teacher Experience Summary

Teachers holding BA degree with certification   _____%

Teachers without permanent certificate in area   _____%

Teachers holding a master's degree and certificate   _____%

Teachers holding a higher degree (EdS or EdD or PhD)   _____%

Teachers in their first year of service   _____%

Teachers with 1–5 years of experience   _____%

Teachers with 6–20 years of experience   _____%

Teachers with more than 20 years of experience   _____%

Teacher identified in-service needs   1st_____

2nd _____

3rd_____

4th_____

5th _____

Teachers planning to move or retire at the end of year   _____%

R8—Life Skills for Students

Place checkmark next to those life skills that we should be teaching our students:

Achievement		**Healthy Habits**	
Improve test scores	____	Smoking and drug awareness	____
Reduce D's and F's	____	Walking for health	____
Fewer notes to parents	____	Participate in intramurals	
Reduction in retentions	____	Awareness of physical growth	____
Raise GPAs	____		
More honor roll students	____	**Stress Reduction**	
Meet needs of achievers	____	Decrease visits to counselor	____
Read designated books	____	Decrease classroom outbursts	____
Develop personal library	____	Decrease acts of aggression	____
Responsibility			
On time to class	____	**Organization of Students**	
Decrease vandalism	____	Bring materials to class	____
Decrease discipline count	____	Complete homework	____
Admit wrongdoing	____	Maintain personal calendar	____
Respect for Others		Bring gym clothes	____
Decrease sarcasm and put downs	____	Manage time wisely	____
Increase sensitivity for others	____	Ask questions to clarify	____
Increase helping others	____	**Problem Solving**	
Attitudinal		Apply learning to real world	____
Exhibit enthusiasm for school	____	Learn in hands-on manner	____
Participate in school activities	____	Solve word problems	____
Join service clubs	____	Possible critical think skills	____
Introduce self to adults	____		
Dress neatly, well-groomed	____		
Know etiquette	____		
Belong to academic club	____		

R9—Standards Status Check

School Computer Standard

	Yes	No
1. Microcomputers in all classrooms?		
2. Qualified technology teacher present?		
3. Two labs with 20 stand-alone computers?		
4. All students scheduled for instruction?		
5. Each teacher has 24-hour access to laptop?		
6. Service agreements in place?		

If any item above is checked "No," describe below the remedy for this deficiency:

What is required to remove "No"?

Who is responsible for this activity?

When is the action to be completed?

Please notify assistant principal for curriculum when activity is completed.

R10—Needs Assessment Outline

General Information

a. Location of school

b. Demographics of surrounding community

c. Natural resources of region

d. Commercial–industrial data

e. Income level of local residents (Chamber of Commerce index)

f. Special socioeconomic considerations

General Population Characteristics

a. Population growth patterns

b. Age, race, or population

c. Education level of population

d. Project population 20 years ahead

School Population Characteristics

a. School enrollment by grade

b. Birthrate trends in school district

c. Immigration, emigration patterns

d. Racial/gender/religious composition of district

Program and Course Offerings in District

a. Organization of school programs

b. Program concept and rationale

c. Course offerings

d. Special program needs

Professional Staff

a. Training and experience

b. Awareness of trends and developments

c. Attitudes toward change

Instructional Patterns and Techniques

a. Philosophical focus of instructional program

b. Awareness of instructional strategies in use

c. Instructional materials in use

d. Grouping for instruction

e. Classroom management techniques

f. Grading and placement of pupils

g. Evaluation of instructional effectiveness

Student Data

a. Student achievement

b. Student experience levels

c. Student self-esteem levels

Facilities

a. Age of facility

b. Use of existing facility

R11—Instructional Planning Cycle

Phase 1

a. Review all curriculum plans

b. State and select instructional objectives

c. Organize content by time

Phase 2

a. Assess student abilities

b. Determine relevance to student lives

c. Reform objectives if necessary

Phase 3

a. Consider appropriate methodologies to meet objectives

b. Review existing knowledge base of students

Phase 4

a. Implement instructional strategies

b. Make corrections as appropriate

Phase 5

a. Select assessment devices

b. Collect evidence of student growth

Phase 6

a. Judge success of strategies

b. Make planning adjustments

c. Match outcome to student experience

R12—Questions to Focus Instruction

1. Is the classroom physically prepared? Is the furniture arrangement appropriate?

2. Is there a plan for getting students into the room and in their seats?

3. Is there a motivational "opener" to smooth the transition from class to class?

4. Can you give the students a preview (advanced organizers) of today's lesson?

5. Have you estimated the time for each activity or lesson section?

6. Will today's activities accomplish the objectives of today's lesson?

7. Do the teaching lessons contain the exact information you want to teach?

8. Has there been thought of the degree of affect in this lesson?

9. Will each student be able to participate at his or her level of learning?

10. Are the necessary and appropriate materials in the classroom today?

11. Do you have a plan for discussion? Has time been allowed for discussion?

12. Have you planned for relevance? Are there real-life examples in the lesson?

13. Have you considered the procedures for handouts and collecting homework?

14. How will special students be involved in today's lesson?

15. Will you use grouping today? How did you choose this pattern?

16. Do you have a plan for any deviant student behavior?

17. Is there a certain standard to be reinforced by today's homework?

18. What kind of test question will you ask about today's material?

19. What technique will you use to close today's class?

20. What is the procedure for class dismissal?

R13—Curriculum Development Cycle

Analysis Stage

1. Identify school philosophy.
2. Search for any board policy relative to intended change.
3. Gain written or public endorsement from superiors.
4. Estimate time frame for project implementation.
5. Form centralized coordinating group (school curriculum team).
6. Delineate anticipated tasks and who will be responsible for what.
7. Conduct needs assessment.
8. Structure awareness sessions with key groups.

Design Stage

1. Translate philosophy into goal statements, standards, and objectives.
2. Project preliminary resource needs and budget.
3. Prioritize goals for project (decision criteria).
4. Block out 2–4 year plan for project.
5. Establish communication and information plan to monitor progress.
6. Establish evaluation targets and design review checks.
7. Develop preliminary staff development plan.
8. Develop final management plan using PERT/CPM approach.

Implementation Stage

1. Provide advanced notice (simple plan) to all interested persons.
2. Provide school(s) with resource kit, glossary, and data from needs assessment.
3. Activate school curriculum team with activity pages describing tasks to be accomplished.
4. Begin staff development in order of importance to curriculum project.
5. Provide local budget supplement based on curriculum plan and timing.

Evaluation Stage

1. Conduct formative evaluation (validation of action) every eight weeks.
2. Conduct major review at six months and revise timelines if necessary.
3. Provide superiors with written summary of progress every eight weeks.

R14—Program Cost Estimates		
Item	*Start-Up Cost*	*Continuing Cost*

A. Personnel
   1. Teachers
   2. Instructional aides
   3. Secretary and bookkeeper
   4. Program coordinator		

B. Fixed Charges
   1. Teacher retirement
   2. Social security
		20%

C. Materials
   1. Start-up only
   2. Replenishment		

D. Equipment
   1. Short-term needs
   2. Long-term needs		

E. Facilities
   1. Renovations
   2. Permanent		

F. Maintenance
   1. Contracts
   2. Special events		

G. Staff Development
   1. Consultant fees
   2. Materials and equipment		

Subtotal		

R15—Sample Activity Page

Goal The school will implement technology that will provide students and staff with the equipment to be productive members of a technologically advanced society.

Objectives

a. Provide each teacher with a laptop computer for 24-hour use.

b. Develop a vocational technology laboratory.

c. Train staff and students in computer usage.

d. House computers throughout the school to assist instruction.

Strategies

a. Provide computer in-service training to all building personnel.

b. Ask community leaders to sponsor some technologies.

c. Contract rather than purchase hardware and software.

Resources

a. School curriculum team will develop a technology plan.

b. Use district staff for writing grant proposals.

c. Use the teachers-training-teachers model with supplemental consultants for in-service training.

d. Form educational partnerships with other schools and business.

Timeline

a. Every teacher will be provided a computer by 20XX.

b. Vocational computer lab to be operational by 20XX.

c. Networking capabilities for instruction operational by 20XX

d. Progress assessment and re-design scheduled for 20XX.

Evaluation

a. Deliver evaluation reports periodically by objective.

b. School curriculum team will oversee teacher training program.

c. Deliver reports to school community via school Web page.

R16—Measure of Student Achievement and Growth

Student Achievement Measures

Achievement tests

Academic aptitude tests

Reading tests (comprehension and vocabulary)

Subject achievement tests

Emotional and social adjustment tests

Writing sample inventories

Work habit and skill measures

Growth Measures

Health assessments

Student self-report

Development of social attitudes

Development of social sensitivity

Development of personal philosophy

Mental health instruments

Displayed creativity

R17—Teacher Practices Inventory

The following teacher practices are observed in the classroom on a regular basis:

Personal Manner

_____ Student work is displayed in the room

_____ Teacher-made bulletin boards (noncommercial)

_____ Seating patterns other than straight rows

_____ Living objects (plants, animals) found in room

_____ Teacher moves about the room freely while instructing

_____ Teacher calls students by name without difficulty

_____ Constructive student-to-student conversations allowed

_____ Teacher uses specific praise and encourages student comments

Individualized

_____ Multilevel texts and materials present

_____ Some students engaged in independent study during class

_____ Students are working on assignments in small, irregular groups

_____ Student work folders and e-portfolios used by teacher to manage learning

_____ Multiple evaluation measures used for same assignment

Displayed Skills

_____ One-to-one conference with students during class

_____ Uses diverse methods during same class period

_____ Small group work during most classes

_____ Teachers at varying level of difficulty around one idea or concept

_____ Stylized learning materials used in class

_____ Uses real life examples when teaching

_____ References student interests or needs during instruction

_____ Maintains classroom discipline without punitive measures

_____ Works with other teachers across subject lines

_____ Teaches general learning skills during subject lessons

_____ Creates instructional materials on his or her own

_____ Uses questioning techniques that encourage participation

R18—Sample Support Document

Topic :   Middle school intramurals

Describe: It is proposed that this middle school sponsor an intramural league featuring activities to encourage physical fitness and social cohesion.

Rationale: Students in the middle school represent the widest range of development in the schooling years. Traditional athletic programs favor those students who have matured early and use their height and weight advantages to excel in sports. Many middle school students learn to be passive observers during this period. Those same students often disassociate from other school activities.

Documentation:

a. Johns Hopkins Preadolescent Studies showing range of physical, social, emotional, and intellectual development.

b. School records indicating declining participation in school-sponsored events from 6th to 8th grade.

c. Notes from teacher visit to Carter Middle School.

R19—Sample Research Summary

Area: Gender bias

Summary: A major concern of educators for more than 20 years, gender bias is present in most schools. This inclination to give preference that interferes with an impartial judgment due to "sex classification" appears to be a two-way street. Major studies have documented sex bias against boys in the elementary grades and against girls at all levels of schooling. Of chief concern in the low performance of girls on achievement tests like the SAT.

Although there has been much progress in ensuring that learning materials are bias-free, and that access is available to girls in all areas of school life, there is still much work to be done. It appears that teacher behaviors and perceptions are the key to minimizing this influence in classrooms.

Key studies:

American Association of University Women. (1992). Shortchanging girls, shortchanging America: A call to action. In *Initiative for educational equity*. Wellesley, MA: Author.

Bennett, R. (1993). Influence of behavior, perception, and gender on teacher judgments of student academic skills. *Journal of Educational Psychology, 85*(2), 347–356.

Sadker, M., & Sadker, D. (1994). *Failing at fairness: How America's schools cheat girls.* New York: Charles Scribner.

R20—Teacher Mini-grant Application

Date: _____

Name: _____

School: _____

Grant Topic:

Brief description of your grant activity:

Budget Amount:

— Equipment

— Materials

— Travel

— Other

Brief description of what you hope to accomplish:

R21—Exceptional Education Laws

Key laws governing the exceptional student in the classroom include:

Public Law 94–142, The Education of All Handicapped Children Act

6 principles:
1. Zero reject must be provided free education ages 3-21

2. Nondiscriminatory evaluation: full evaluation before placement

3. IEP: individualized education program defining student experience

4. LRE: must be placed in the least restricted environment possible

5. Due process: decisions about the student can be challenged in law

6. Parent participation: parents may refuse the designated program

This act also identified types of disability such as educable mentally handicapped, hearing-impaired, specific learning disabilities (SLD), and emotionally handicapped (EH). Most public school students are categorized as SLD or EH.

IDEA (1990), The Individuals with Disabilities Education Act

A second major bill influencing care of exceptional students in schools, the Individuals with Disabilities Education Act, changes the rules for placing ESE (exceptional student education) students in the classroom. It states that

"children with disabilities will be educated with children without disabilities and that no separate channels should be supported except under the direst circumstances."

R22—Teacher Deployment for Inclusion

Depending on the experience of your teachers and the number of exceptional students in your school, you may wish to consider three patterns for using special education teachers.

Collaboration Model: direct interaction between at least two coequal teachers (regular and special teachers) who voluntarily engage in shared decision making as they work toward common goals.

Collaborative Consultation Model: A special education teacher provides only strategies and consultation to several regular education teachers. All of the exceptional students are included in the regular room.

Co-Teaching Model: A regular teacher and a special teacher share equally on a full-time basis the responsibilities of teaching regular and special education students in the same classroom.

R23—Adult Learning Strategies

Delivering staff development to adults requires thought about the age and stage of the individual teacher. A 22-year-old is quite different from a 50-year-old, and the way they receive training should be appropriate to their experience and skill development.

Age 20–30	Because this teacher has been a student most of his or her life, a formal format, with lecture and tests, is appropriate. This teacher will have limited skills and requires additional credentialing. There will be little fear of at-home learning via the computer. Motivation is to "get going."
Age 30–40	This teacher is secure, having mastered the survival stage and been awarded a continuing contract. A less formal format is called for, with greater opportunity to socialize and learn from other teachers. Motivation is self-expansion.
Age 40–50	Teachers in this age range are secure, having taught 20 years or more. Most training will have been "seen before." Look for some recreational learners (social beings) and they may have short attention spans. The instruction is best delivered by peers, and time is very precious to this learner. Materials should be classroom-ready and use a larger font. Motivation is general growth, adult interests.
Age 50-60	This teacher will have a rich teaching life to call on and is generally very positive about training. Learning will occur most readily in a tutorial or small-group format. This learner does not like evaluation and may fear failure in front of others. Motivation is leadership due to long experience.

Resource B

Standard Curriculum Planning Resources

Citizens' Organizations

Council for Basic Education
1319 F Street, NW
Washington, DC 20004-1152
E-mail: lsamotshozo@usaid.gov

National Coalition for Children
6542 Hitt Street
McLean, VA 22101

National Congress of Parents and Teachers
1715 25th Street
Rock Island, IL 61201

Education Professional Organizations and Associations

American Association for Higher Education
2020 Pennsylvania Avenue, NW
Suite 975
Washington, DC 20006
www.aahea.org

American Association of School Administrators
801 N. Quincy Street
Suite 700
Arlington, VA 22203-1730
www.aasa.org

American Council on Education
One Dupont Circle, NW
Washington, DC 20036
www.acenet.edu

American Educational Research Association
1230 17th Street, NW
Washington, DC 20036
www.aera.net

Association for Career and Technical Education
1510 H Street, NW
Washington, DC 20005

Association for Supervision and Curriculum Development (ASCD)
1703 North Beauregard Street
Alexandria, VA 22311-1714
www.ascd.org

Children's Television Workshop
One Lincoln Plaza
New York, NY 10023
www.ctw.org

College Entrance Examination Board
888 7th Avenue
New York, NY 10019
www.collegeboard.org

Council for American Private Education
13017 Wisteria Dr. #457
Germantown, MD 20874
www.capenet.org

Council of Chief State School Officers
One Massachusetts Avenue, NW
Suite 700
Washington, DC 20001-1431
www.ccsso.org

International Reading Association
800 Barksdale Road
Newark, DE 19711-3269

Joint Council on Economic Education
1212 Avenue of the Americas
New York, NY 10036

National Art Education Association
1916 Association Drive
Reston, VA 20191-1590
www.naea-reston.org

National Association for Education of Young Children
1313 L Street, NW
Suite 500
Washington, DC 20005
www.naeyc.org

National Association of Elementary School Principals
1615 Duke Street
Alexandria, VA 22314
www.naesp.org

National Association for Public Continuing Adult Education
1201 16th Street, NW
Washington, DC 20036

National Association of Secondary School Principals
1904 Association Drive
Reston, VA 22091-1537
www.nassp.org

National Council of Teachers of English
1111 Kenyon Road
Urbana, IL 61801-1096
www.ncte.org

National Council of Teachers of Mathematics
1906 Association Drive
Reston, VA 20191-9988
www.nctm.org

National Education Association
1201 16th Street, NW
Washington, DC 20036
www.nea.org

National Middle School Association
4151 Executive Parkway
Suite 300
Westerville, OH 43081
www.nmsa.org

National School Boards Association
1680 Duke Street
Alexandria, VA 22314
www.nsba.org

National Science Teachers Association
1840 Wilson Blvd.
Arlington, VA 22201-3000
www.nsta.org

Ethnic and Minority Organizations
Bilingual Education Service Center
500 South Dwyer
Arlington Heights, IL 60005

National Council of Negro Women, Inc.
633 Pennsylvania Avenue
Washington, DC 20004
www.ncnw.org

National Indian Education Association
110 Maryland Avenue, NE
Suite 104
Washington, DC 20002
www.niea.org

National Organization for Women (NOW)
733 15th Street, NW
2nd Floor
Washington, DC 20005
www.now.org

Federal Agencies

House of Representatives
Washington, DC 20515
www.house.gov

National Institute of Education
555 New Jersey Avenue, NW
Washington, DC 20208

National Science Foundation
4201 Wilson Blvd.
Arlington, VA 22230
www.nsf.gov

U.S. Department of Education
400 Maryland Avenue, SW
Washington, DC 20202-0498
www.ed.gov

U.S. Senate
Washington, DC 20510
www.senate.gov

General Associations

Committee for Economic Development
2000 L Street, NW
Suite 700
Washington, DC 20036
www.ced.org

National Urban League
120 Wall Street
New York, NY 10005
www.nul.org

Labor Organizations
American Federation of Teachers
555 New Jersey Avenue, NW
Washington, DC 20001
www.aft.org

Resource C

Curriculum Resource Sites on the Internet

Mapping and Methodology Sites

Concept mapping tutorial: http://ltsnpsy.york.ac.uk/conceptmapping/conceptmapping/html/tutorial

Online organizers and concept maps: http://www.graphic.org/concept.html

Reading Quest: http://curry.edschool.virginia.edu/go/readquest/strat/

Continuous Progress: A Districtwide Educational Program: http://www.continuousprogress.org

Geocities Multi-age Continuous Progress Links and Resources: http://www.geocities.com/EnchantedForest/Glade/6190/multiage.html

Multi-age Continuous Progress: http://projects.sd3.k12.nf.ca/multiage/multiage.htm

Smoothing Rough Edges in Concrete: http://projects.sd3.k12.nf.ca/multiage/multiage.htm

Cooperative Learning

Basic Elements of Cooperative Learning: http://www.ericdigests.org/1995-1/elements.htm

Benefits of Collaborative Learning: http://www.gdrc.org/kmgmt/c-learn/44.html

Cooperative Learning: http://www.ed.gov/pubs/OR/ConsumerGuides/cooplear.html

Cooperative Learning Classroom Compass: http://www.sedl.org/scimath/compass/v01n02/welcome.html

Cooperative Learning e-Book: http://home.capecod.net/~tpanitz/ebook/contents.html

Elements of Cooperative Learning: http://edtech.kennesaw.edu/intech/cooperativelearning.htm

Jigsaw Learning Links: http://www.jigsaw.org/links.htm

Teamworks: Skills for Collaborative Work: http://www.vta.spcomm.uiuc.edu/

Differentiated Instruction

A Different Place differentiated curriculum and practice in Kansas: http://www.adifferentplace.org/differentiated.htm

A Questioning Toolkit, by Jamie McKenzie: http://questioning.org/Q7/toolkit.html

Curriculum Compacting: http://www.montgomeryschoolsmd.org/curriculum/enriched/giftedprograms/curriculumcompacting.shtm

Curriculum Differentiation Academic Challenge: http://www.learnerslink.com/curriculum.htm

Curriculum Differentiation Wilmette Public Schools: http:www.wilmette39.org/DI39/

Differentiating Instruction for Advanced Learners in the Mixed-Ability Middle School ERIC Classroom Carol Tomlinson: http:www.cast.org/publications/ncac/ncac_diffinstruc.html

Differentiation in Manteno, Illinois, Schools: http://www.manteno.k12.il.us/curriculumdiff/

Differentiation With Literature Circles: http://www.manteno.k12.il.us/curriculumdiff/literature_circles.htm

Focus on Differentiated Instruction: http://www.ascd.org/handbook/demo/ctq/8spr00.html

Leadership for Differentiated Classrooms Carol Tomlinson, AASA: http:www.ascd.org/portal/site/ascd/menuitem.3adeebc6736780dddeb3ffdb62108a0c/

Mapping a Route Toward Differentiated Instruction: http://pdonline.ascd.org/pd_online/diffinstr/el199909_tomlinson.html

Electronic Learning

Computer-Based Technology and Learning: Evolving Uses and Expectations: http://www.ncrel.org/sdrs/areas/techbib.htm

Edutopia, The George Lucas Foundation and Education: http://www.glef.org/

International Society for Technology in Education (ISTE): http://www.iste.org/

Laptops and Learning: http://www.techteachers.com/laptops.htm

Maine Learning Technology Initiative: http://www.state.me.us/mlte/

Research on Technology Implementation of the Endeavour Group: http://www.theendeavourgroup.net/research.html

Teaching With Laptops: Exemplary Lessons: http://www.nsta.org/publications/interactive/laptop/teach/exemplary.htm

Technology Integration: http://www.education-world.com/index.shtml#Technology

Technology Integration: What's Working for K-12 Schools: http://www.glef.org/php/keyword.php?id=137

The Impact of Technology on Student Learning: http://www.apple.com/au/education/k12/onetoone/research.html

Integrated Curriculum

http://www.ericfacility.net/databases/ERIC Digests/ed351095.html

Integrated Curriculum, Northwest Regional Educational Laboratory: http://www.nwrel.org

Integrated Curriculum: http://ncrve.berkeley.edu/ST2.1/TowardanIntegrated.html

Integrated Curriculum Design Packet Downloadable Handbook: http://apps.sdhc.k12.fl.us/public/mainindex/information/

Meaningful, Engaged Learning: http://www.ncrel.org/sdrs/engaged.htm

New Visions for Teaching and Learning in the 21st Century: http://www.thecommittedsardine.net/infosavvy/education/handouts/nvfl.pdf

Planning Integrated Curriculum: The Call to Adventure (the first two chapters of Susan Drake's book from ASCD): http://www.ascd.org/ed_topics/1993drake/1993draketoc.html

Learning Styles

Education and Learning Styles: http://www.Idpride.net/learning styles.MI.htm

Index to Learning Styles: http://www.chaminade.org/inspire/learnstl.htm

Learning Styles and Multiple Intelligences: http://www.ldpride.net/learningstyles.MI.htm

Learning Styles Handbook: http://www.d.umn.edu/student/loon/acad/strat/lrnsty.html

Looping

American Association of School Administrators: In the Loop: http://www.ncrel.org/sdrs/areas/issues/methods/instrctn/in5lk10.htm

Implementing Looping: http://www.educationworld.com/a_admin/admin/admin120.shtml

In the Loop: Teachers and Students Progressing Together: http://www.education-world.com/a_admin/admin120.shtml

Looping: Adding Time, Strengthening Relationships: http://www.ericfacility.net/databases/ERIC_Digests/ed414098.html

Looping as a Class Placement Approach: http://www.salmonbay.seattleschools.org/fac/Looping.htm

Looping Two Years with the Same Class: http://findarticles.com/p/articles/mi_qa3617/is_199810/ai_n8824524

Mentoring

Andrew Jackson Middle School's Unique Mentoring Program: http://schools.pgcps.org/sip/6444.pdf

DeKalb County's Partners Pals Mentoring Program: http://www.dekalb.k12.ga.us/instruction/mentoring/

e-Mentoring at Cargill-Olseon Middle School: http://www.cargill.com/commun/email.htm

Foundations of Successful Youth Mentoring: http://www.nwrel.org/mentoring/pdf/foundations.pdf

Mentoring Edutopia: http://www.glef.org/php/keyword.php?id=228

Mentoring Programs: http://ncrve.berkeley.edu/abstracts/MDS-771/MDS-771-Mentorin.html

Mentoring Programs That Work: http://www.education-world.com/aadmin/admin261.shtml

Sligo Middle School Team Mentoring Program: http://www.webpronews.com/topnews/2004/09/29/aol-awards-grants-to-middle-and-high-schools

Multiple Intelligences

Intelligences for the New Millennium: http://portal.acm.org/citation.cfm?id=779343

Mrs. Young's Page on Multiple Intelligences: http://www.fortunecity.com/millenium/garston/49/multiintell.html

Technology and Multiple Intelligences: http://eduscapes.com/tap/topic68.htm

Walter McKenzie's Multiple Intelligence Pages: http://surfaquarium.com/MI/

Multi-Age and Nongraded

Building Support for Multi-age Education: http://eric.ed.gov/ERICWebPortal/recordDetail?accno=ED409604

Developmentally Appropriate Practice: http://www.ericfacility.net/ericdigests.ed413106.html

Enhancing Learning Through Multi-age Grouping: http://www.ncrel.org/sdrs/areas/issues/methods/instrctn/in500.htm

Multi-age Classrooms: Still Evolving: http://www.edletter.org/past/issues/1998-jf/multiage.shtml

Multi-age Education.Com: http://www.multiage-education.com/

Multi-age Links to Resources and Research: http://www.multiage-education.com/multiagelinks/

Multi-age Thesis Paper and Resource Links: http://www.multiage-info.com/

Multi-age: Time for a Change: http://wsd.waupaca.k12.wi.us/wlc/primary/multi/multigrad.html

Providing Authentic Multi-Level Instruction: http://www.wholeschooling.net/WS/WSPrncples/WS%203%20Multilevel.html

Problem-Based Learning

Illinois Mathematics and Science Academy's Center for Problem Based Learning: http://www2.imsa.edu/programs/pbl/cpbl.html

Internet Classrooms Problem Based Learning: http://www.imsa.edu/programs/pbln/

Power Learning Creating Student-Centered Problem Based Classrooms: http://www.fnopress.com/PLOZ

Problem Based Learning: http://www.udel.edu/pbl/

Project Based Learning at a Glance: http://www.glef.org/php/keyword.php?id=037

Service Learning

Introduction to Service Learning for Middle School Students: http://www.macomb.k12.mi.us/WQ/meb2cl.htm

Learning in Deed: http://learningindeed.org/index.html

Middle School Service Learning Resources: http://www.middleschool.net/adminisr/serlearn.htm

National Service Learning Clearinghouse: http://www.servicelearning.org/

National Youth Leadership Council: http://www.nylc.org/

Service Learning Research and Links: http://learningindeed.org/research/slresearch/

Webquests and Cyber-Guides

Another Webquest Matrix: http://www.cesa8.k12.wi.us/teares/webquestmatrix.htm

Bernie Dodge's Webquest Page: http://webquest.sdsu.edu/

Classic Children's Stories: http://childhoodreading.com/

Cyberguides to Literature: http://www.sdcoe.k12.ca.us/score/cyberguide.html

Kathy Schrock's Guide to Webquests: http://school.discovery.com/schrockguide/webquest/webquest.html

Literature Based Webquests: http://eduscapes.com/ladders/themes/webquests.htm

Webquest Search: http://webquest.org/search/

Resource D

Reading for Greater Understanding

Historical Perspective

R. Callahan   *Education and the Cult of Efficiency* (1962). Chicago: University of Chicago Press.

G. Counts   *Dare the Schools Create a New Social Order* (1932). New York: Doubleday.

L. Cremin   *The Genius of American Education* (1965). Pittsburgh: University of Pittsburg Press.

H. Kliebard   *The Struggle for the American Curriculum* (1986). Boston: Routledge and Kegan.

M. Mead   *The School in the American Culture* (1959). Cambridge: Harvard University Press.

D. Tanner   *The History of the School Curriculum* (1990). New York: Macmillan.

Systems

K. Fast   *Organization and Management: Systems Approach* (1985). Pearson Education.

K. Feyereisen   *Supervision and Curriculum Renewal: Systems Approach* (1973). New York: Appleton-Century-Croft.

Politics

M. Apple   *Ideology and the Curriculum* (1990). New York: Routledge.

P. Freire   *The Politics of Education* (1985). South Hadley, MA: Bergen and Garvey.

A. Wildavsky   *The Politics of the Budgetary Process* (1979). Boston: Little, Brown.

D. Wiles   *Practical Politics for School Administrators* (1979). Boston: Allyn & Bacon.

Philosophy

H. Broudy   *Building a Philosophy of Education* (1961). New York: Routledge.

I. Scheffler   *The Language of Education* (1960). Springfield, IL: Charles C Thomas.

Learning Theory

J. Bruner   *Toward a Theory of Instruction* (1967). Cambridge: Harvard University Press.

J. Dewey   *The Child and the Curriculum* (1902). Indianapolis: Bobbs-Merrill.

J. Piaget   *The Language and Thought of a Child* (1959). London: Routledge.

N. Shedroff   *Experience Design* (2001). London: New Riders.

Curriculum Theory

H. Taba   *Curriculum Development: Theory Into Practice* (1962). New York: Harcourt, Brace, Jovanovich.

R. Tyler   *Basic Principles of Curriculum and Instruction* (1949). Chicago: University of Chicago Press.

Teaching

M. McLuhan   *The Medium Is the Message* (1967). New York: Bantam.

J. McNeil   *The Essentials of Teaching* (1990). Boston: Macmillan.

B. F. Skinner   *The Technology of Teaching* (1968). New York: Vintage.

Knowledge

B. Bloom   *Taxonomy I: The Cognitive Domain* (1956). New York: David McKay.

J. Bruner   *On Knowing* (1962). Cambridge: Harvard University Press.

E. D. Hirsch   *Cultural Literacy* (1987). New York: Random House.

Human Relations

A. Combs	*Perceiving, Behaving, Becoming* (1962). Alexandria, VA: ASCD.
G. Homans	*The Human Group* (1950). New York: Harcourt, Brace.
R. Katz	The Social Dynamic of Groups (1966, Jan/Feb). *Harvard Business Review.*
M. Sherif	*Reference Groups* (1964). New York: Harper Brothers.

Leadership

S. Covey	*The Seven Habits of Highly Effective People* (1990). New York: Simon & Schuster.
P. Drucker	*The Effective Executive* (1967). New York: HarperCollins.
T. Jacobs	*Leadership and Exchange in Formal Organizations* (1970). Alexandria, VA: Human Resources Organization.
R. Stogdill	*Handbook of Leadership* (1974). New York: Free Press.

Change Theory

W. Bennis	*The Planning of Change* (1985). New York: Holt, Rinehart, Winston.
H. Lionberger	*Adoption of New Ideas and Practice* (1960). Ames: Iowa State University Press.
E. Rogers	*Diffusion of Innovations* (2003). New York: Free Press.
J. Wiles	*Promoting Change in Schools: Ground Level Practices That Work* (1993). New York: Scholastic, Inc.

Research

J. Creswell	*Education Research: Conducting, and Evaluating Quantitative and Qualitative Research* (2007). Upper Saddle River, NJ: Prentice Hall.
R. Mager	*Goal Analysis* (1972). Belmont, CA: Fearon Press.
J. Popham	*Educational Evaluation* (1975). Boston: Allyn & Bacon.

Resource E

Glossary

Ability grouping: Organizing pupils into homogeneous groups according to intellectual ability for instruction.

Accountability: Holding schools and teachers responsible for what students learn.

Accreditation: Recognition given to an educational institution after it has met accepted standards applied to it by an outside agency.

Achievement test: Standardized test designed to measure how much has been learned from a particular subject.

Affective domain: Attitudinal and emotional areas of learning, such as values and feelings.

Aligned: A term used to indicate that a school curriculum is matched with state and national standards as well as with state and national tests.

Balanced curriculum: Incorporates essential learning skills, subject content, and personal development.

Behavioral approach: An approach that focuses on observable behaviors instead of on internal events such as thinking and emotions.

Behavioral objective: Precise statement of what the learner must do to demonstrate mastery at the end of a prescribed learning task.

Block scheduling: The reorganization of the daily or annual school schedule to allow students and teachers to have larger, more concentrated segments of time each day, week, or grading period on each subject. *See also* modular scheduling.

Cognitive domain: In Bloom's taxonomy, memory and reasoning objectives.

Cognitive learning: Academic learning of subject matter.

Competency: The demonstrated ability to perform specified acts at a particular level of skill or accuracy.

Competency-based instruction: Instructional programming that measures learning through the demonstration of predetermined outcomes. Mastery is assessed through an evaluation of the process as well as the product.

Cooperative learning: Two or more students working together on a learning task.

Core (fused) curriculum: Integration of two or more subjects; for example, English and social studies. Problem and theme orientations often serve as the integrating design. *See also* interdisciplinary program.

Criterion-referenced evaluation: Evaluation that measures success by the attainment of established levels of performance. Individual success is based wholly on the performance of the individual without regard to the performance of others.

Curriculum: The total experiences planned for a school or students.

Curriculum alignment: Matching learning activities with desired outcomes, or matching what is taught with what is tested.

Curriculum guide: A written statement of objectives, content, and activities to be used with a particular subject at specified grade levels; usually produced by state departments of education or local education agencies.

Curriculum management planning: A systematic method of planning for change.

Departmentalization: The division of instructional staff, resources, and classes by academic disciplines, service delivery models such as separate general and special education programming, or some other arbitrary structure for compartmentalization.

Developmental tasks: Social, physical, maturational tasks regularly encountered by all individuals in our society as they progress from childhood to adolescence.

Educational goals: A statement of expectations for students or a school program.

Essential learning skills: Basic skills, such as reading, listening, and speaking, that are introduced in the elementary school and reinforced in the middle and high school.

Feedback: Evidence from student responses and reactions that indicates the degree of success in achieving lesson objectives. Teachers seek feedback by way of discussion, student questions, written exercises, and test returns.

Flexible scheduling: Provisions in scheduling allowing for variance in length of time, order, or rotation of classes.

Formative evaluation: A method of assessment that occurs before or during instruction to (a) guide teacher planning or (b) identify students' needs.

Goals, educational: Desired learning outcomes stated for a group of students and requiring anywhere from several weeks to several years to attain.

Graded school system: A division of schools into groups of students according to the curriculum or the ages of pupils, as in the six elementary grades.

Heterogeneous grouping: Student grouping that does not divide learners on the basis of ability or academic achievement.

Homogeneous grouping: Student grouping that divides learners on the basis of specific levels of ability, achievement, or interest. Sometimes referred to as *tracking.*

House plan: Type of organization in which the school is divided into units ("houses"), with each having an identity and containing the various grades and, in large part, its own faculty. The purpose of a house plan is to achieve decentralization (closer student–faculty relationships) and easier and more flexible team-teaching arrangements.

Independent study: Work performed by students without the direct supervision of the teacher to develop self-study skills and to expand and deepen interests.

Individualized education program (IEP): A mechanism through which a child's special needs are identified; goals, objectives, and services are outlined; and methods for evaluating progress are delineated.

Individualized instruction: Instruction that focuses on the interests, needs, and achievements of individual learners.

Innovations: New instructional strategies, organizational designs, building rearrangements, equipment uses, or materials from which improved learning results are anticipated.

In-service education: Continuing education for teachers who are actually teaching, or who are in service.

Interdisciplinary program: Instruction that integrates and combines subject matter ordinarily taught separately into a single organizational structure.

Interdisciplinary team: Combination of teachers from different subject areas who plan and conduct coordinated lessons in those areas for particular groups of pupils. Common planning time, flexible scheduling, and cooperation and communication among team teachers are essential to interdisciplinary teaming.

Interscholastic program: Athletic activities or events whose primary purpose is to foster competition among schools and school districts. Participation usually is limited to students with exceptional athletic ability.

Intramural (intrascholastic) program: Athletic activities or events held during the school day, or shortly thereafter, whose primary purpose is to encourage all students to participate regardless of athletic ability.

Learning: A change of behavior as a result of experience.

Least restrictive environment: The program best suited to meet the special needs of a child with a disability while keeping the child as close as possible to the regular educational program.

Mainstreaming: A plan by which exceptional children receive special education in the regular classroom as much of the time as possible.

Middle school: A school between elementary and high school, housed separately, ideally in a building designed for its purpose, and covering usually three of the middle school years, beginning with Grade 5 or 6.

Minicourses: Special interest (enrichment) activities of short duration that provide learning opportunities based on student interest, faculty expertise, and community involvement; also called *exploratory courses, short-interest-centered courses,* or *electives.*

Modular Scheduling: Modular scheduling uses fixed time units (15 minutes) and allocates some number of "mods" to a subject (i.e., 3 mods = 45 minute period). This type of scheduling provides flexibility.

Need-structured approach: A learning theory concerned with the needs and drives of students that seeks to use such natural motivational energy to promote learning.

Nongraded school: A type of school organization in which grade lines are eliminated for a sequence of two or more years.

Norm-referenced grading: Evaluating a student's performance by comparing it with the performance of others.

Paraprofessional: A person employed by a school, program, or district to assist a certified professional and extend the services provided to the students. The paraprofessional may have entry-level training but is not a fully licensed educator or therapist.

Performance objective: Targeted outcome measures for evaluating the learning of particular process-based skills and knowledge.

Portfolio, learner's: A diversified combination of samples of a student's quantitative and qualitative work.

Readiness: The point at which a student is intellectually, physically, or socially able to learn a concept or exhibit a particular behavior.

Scope: The parameters of learning; for example, a subject-matter discipline sets its own scope, often by grade level.

Self-contained classroom: A form of classroom organization in which the same teacher conducts all or nearly all of the instruction in all or most subjects in the same classroom for all or most of the school day.

Sequence: The organization of an area of study. Frequently the organization is chronological, moving from simple to complex. Some sequences are spiraled, using structure, themes, or concept development as guidelines. A few schools use persistent life situations to shape sequence.

Staff development: A body of activities designed to improve the proficiencies of the educator–practitioner.

Subject content: A type of curriculum that stresses the mastery of subject matter, with all other outcomes considered subsidiary. Also called *subject-matter curriculum. See also* homogeneous grouping.

Support personnel: Ancillary personnel such as guidance, media, custodial, clerical, and social services persons who help facilitate the instructional program.

Teachers Training Teachers (TTT): An in-service process by which teachers receive instruction from peers, usually at the school level.

Team teaching: A plan by which several teachers, organized into a team with a leader, provide the instruction for a larger group of children than would usually be found in a self-contained classroom.

Tracking: The method of grouping students according to their ability level in homogeneous classes or learning experiences.

Unstructured time: Periods of time during the school day that have not been designated for a specific purpose and that present students with less supervision. The time between finishing lunch and the bell to return to the classroom is an example of unstructured time.

Suggested Reading

American Association of School Administrators. (1996, Spring). What research says about student assessment. *Improving America's Schools: A Newsletter on Issues in School Reform.* Retrieved on May 4, 2008, from http://www.ed.gov./IASA/newsletters/assess/pt4.html

Broudy, H. (1962), *Building a philosophy of education.* New York: Harcourt, Brace.

Castetter, W. (2000). *The human resource function in educational administration.* Upper Saddle River, NJ: Prentice Hall.

Drake, S., & Burns, R. (2004). *Meeting standards through integrated curriculum.* Alexandria, VA: Association for Supervision and Curriculum Development.

Eisner, E. (2002). *The educational imagination: On the design and evaluation of school programs.* Upper Saddle River, NJ: Prentice Hall.

Goodlad, J. (2004). *A place called school.* New York: McGraw-Hill.

Jacobs, H. (2004). *Getting results with curriculum mapping.* Alexandria, VA: Association for Supervision and Curriculum Development.

Jacobs, T. (1970). *Leadership and exchange in formal organizations.* Alexandria, VA: Human Resource Research Organization.

Kimpson, R. (1982, Spring). Employing systematic procedures in goal-setting: A matter of necessity, not choice. *Planning and Changing, 13*(1), 31–47. (ERIC Document Reproduction Service No. EJ262626)

Knowles, M. (1973). *The adult learner: A neglected species.* Houston: Gulf Publishing.

Lionberger, H. (1961). *Adoption of new ideas and practices.* Ames: Iowa State University Press.

Litwin, G., & Stringer, R. (1968). *Motivation and organizational climate.* Boston: Harvard Business School Press.

Lorin, W. A., & Krathwohl, D. (2000). *Taxonomy of learning, teaching, and assessing.* Boston: Allyn & Bacon.

Lovell, J., & Wiles, K. (1983). *Supervision for better schools* (5th ed.). Englewood Cliffs, NJ: Prentice Hall.

Mager, R. (1972). *Goal analysis.* Belmont, CA: Fearon Press.

Maslow. A. (1987). *Motivation and personality.* New York: Harper & Row.

McLuhan, M. (1967). *The medium is the message.* New York: McGraw-Hill.

McNeil, J., & Wiles, J. (1990). *The essentials of teaching.* New York: Macmillan.

Modell, M. (1996). *A professional's guide to systems analysis* (2nd ed.). New York: McGraw-Hill.

Oakes, J. (1985). *Keeping track: How schools structure inequality.* New Haven, CT: Yale University Press.

Parkay, F., & Stanford, B. *Becoming a teacher: Breaking the mold.* New York: McGraw-Hill.

Rogers, E. (2003). *Diffusion of innovations* (5th ed.). New York: Free Press.

Sarason, S. (1971). *The culture of the school and the problem of change.* Boston: Allyn & Bacon.

Slavin, R. (1990). Achievement effects of ability grouping in secondary schools: A best evidence synthesis. *Review of Educational Research, 60,* 471–499.

Stogdill, R. (1974). *Handbook of leadership: A survey of theory and research.* New York: Free Press.

Taylor, A., & Valentine, B. (1985). *What Research Says About Effective Schools, Number 1, Data-Search Reports.* West Haven, CT: NEA Professional Library. (ERIC Document Reproduction Service No. ED274073).

Tucker, P., & Stronge, J. (2005). *Study Guide for Linking Teacher Evaluation and Student Achievement.* Alexandria, Virginia, Association for Supervision and Curriculum Development.

Tyler, R. (1949). *Basic principles of curriculum and instruction.* Chicago: University of Chicago Press.

Udelhofen, S. (2005). *Keys to curriculum mapping.* Thousand Oaks, CA: Corwin Press.

Virginia Beach City Schools. (2004). *Textbook policy and textbook adoption process.* Retrieved May 3, 2008, from http://www.vbschools.com/textbook03.html

Wagner, T., Kegan, R., Lahey, L., Lemons, R. W., Garnier, J., Helsing, D., et al. (2006). *Change leadership: A practical guide to transforming our schools.* New York: Jossey-Bass.

Wiggins, G., & McTighe, J. (2001). *Understanding by design.* Englewood Cliffs, NJ: Prentice Hall.

Wiles, J. (1976). *Planning guidelines for middle school education.* Dubuque, IA: Kendall Hunt.

Wiles, J. (1993). *Promoting change in schools: Ground level practices that work.* New York: Scholastic, Inc.

Wiles, J. (2005). *Curriculum essentials: A resource for educators* (2nd ed.). Boston: Allyn & Bacon.

Wiles, J., & Bondi, J. (2004). *Supervision: A guide to practice* (6th ed.). Upper Saddle River, NJ: Prentice Hall.

Wiles, J., & Bondi, J. (2007). *Curriculum development: A guide to practice* (7th ed.). Upper Saddle River, NJ: Prentice Hall.

Index

CORWIN
PRESS

The Corwin Press logo—a raven striding across an open book—represents the union of courage and learning. Corwin Press is committed to improving education for all learners by publishing books and other professional development resources for those serving the field of PreK–12 education. By providing practical, hands-on materials, Corwin Press continues to carry out the promise of its motto: **"Helping Educators Do Their Work Better."**